Microwave Oven Cookbook

Insta-Matic and Variable Power

Dear Quasar Owner:

Congratulations on your purchase of one of Quasar's new microwave ovens featuring INSTA-MATIC™ Cooking with Humidity Sensor control. INSTA-MATIC Cooking by Quasar ushers in a new era of cooking ease. Now, so many of your everyday recipes can be cooked without a need to guess at power settings, cooking times or temperatures. Quasar takes the guesswork out of microwave meals.

In addition to INSTA-MATIC Cooking, your new Quasar microwave oven is equipped with such features as Custom Cook, Temperature Probe Cooking, Three Stage Memory, Weight and Time Defrost, Auto Start, Custom Cook and Temperature Hold.

This cookbook has been developed, and should be used along with your Owner's Manual, to help you become more familiar with these special features and to get the most pleasure out of your new Quasar Microwave Oven. Information Charts, special helps, test kitchen hints and other quick tips have been included along with the basics of microwave cooking. As with any new learning experience, once you know the fundamentals, all the rest is amazingly simple and easy.

The recipes we share with you are some of our favorites and have been developed by home economists of the Quasar Kitchen. Each recipe uses one or more of the special Quasar features that we are sure you will enjoy using.

Very truly yours,

Quasar Company

Please direct all inquiries to:
Consumer Relations
Quasar Company, Division of Matsushita Electric Corp. of America
9401 W. Grand Ave.
Franklin Park, IL 60131

In Canada:
Quasar Canada, Division of Matsushita Electric of Canada Ltd.
5770 AMBLER DRIVE
MISSISSAUGA, ONTARIO L4W 2T3

Contents

INTRODUCTION
Cooking With Microwave Energy

Microwaves are a form of high frequency radio waves similar to those used by a radio including AM, FM, and CB. They are, however, much shorter than radio waves; approximately four to six inches long with a diameter of about one-fourth inch. Electricity is converted into microwave energy by the magnetron tube. From the magnetron tube, microwave energy is transmitted to the oven cavity where it is: reflected, transmitted and absorbed.

Reflection
Microwaves are reflected by metal just as a ball is bounced off a wall. A combination of stationary (interior walls) and rotating metal (stirrer fan) helps assure that the microwaves are well distributed within the oven cavity to produce even cooking.

Transmission
Microwaves pass through some materials such as paper, glass and plastic much like sunlight shining through a window. Because these substances do not absorb or reflect the microwave energy, they are ideal materials for microwave oven cooking containers.

Absorption
During heating, microwaves will be absorbed by food. They penetrate to a depth of about ¾ to 1½ inches. Microwave energy excites the molecules in the food (especially water, fat and sugar molecules), and causes them to vibrate at a rate of 2,450,000,000 times per second. This vibration causes friction, and heat is produced. If you vigorously rub your hands together, you will feel heat produced by friction. The internal cooking of large foods results from conduction. The heat which is produced by friction is conducted to the center of the food. Foods also continue to cook by conduction during standing time (see page 15.)
Because microwaves dissipate, much like sunlight as it reaches the Earth's surface, they cannot be stored in food.

MICROWAVE COOKING UTENSILS

Microwave cooking opens new possibilities in convenience and flexibility for cooking containers. Although new microwave accessories are constantly being introduced, many utensils readily available in most kitchens may also be used for microwave cooking and heating.

Glass, Ceramic and China

Heat-Resistant glass cookware is invaluable in microwave cooking. Many of these items are readily available in most homes: glass measures, custard cups, mixing bowls, loaf dishes, covered casseroles, oblong baking dishes, pie plates and round or square cake dishes. Examples of this type of cookware are Pyrex®, and Corning Ware®, Fire-King® Ovenware® and Glassbake®.

Dinnerware can be used for microwave cooking. Many brands of dinnerware are microwave safe. Check the care information for reference to microwave use for dinnerware and serving pieces. If dinnerware is marked ovenproof, it frequently is safe to use in the microwave oven. However, to be sure, check by conducting the microwave dish test. Examples of this type of dinnerware are: Corelle®, Temperware® and Denby® dinnerware.

Several types of glassware and dinnerware are not recommended for use in the microwave oven. Remember these basic rules when using dinnerware and glassware. Do not use dishes with metallic trim or containers with metal parts. Arcing may occur and /or the dish may break.
Do not use ceramic mugs or cups with glued-on handles. The handles may fall off with continued heating.
Do not use delicate glassware. Although the glassware may be transparent to microwave energy, the heat from the food may cause the glassware to crack.

Jars and Bottles can be used to warm food to serving temperature, if the lid is removed first. Cooking should not be done in these containers since most are not heat resistant and during extended heating times, heat from food would cause cracking or breaking.

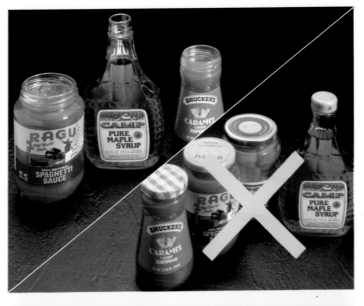

Browning Dishes are used to sear chops, meat patties, steaks etc. A special coating on the bottom of the dish absorbs the microwave energy and becomes very hot. When foods are added to the dish, the result is a seared effect. Preheat dish according to manufacturer's directions. Add food to be seared and cook according to recipe or personal preference.
Use pot holders to remove dish from microwave oven.
Do not use browning dish with temperature probe.
Check information included with browning dish for detailed instructions and heating chart.

How to Test a Container for Safe Microwave Oven Use:

Fill a 1-cup glass measure with water and place it in the microwave oven along with the glass container to be tested; heat one minute at HIGH. If the container is microwave oven safe, it should remain comfortably cool to the touch and the water should be hot. If the container becomes hot, it has absorbed microwave energy and should not be used. This test cannot be used with plastic containers.

Plastics

Plastic Dishes that are safe for microwave cooking are readily available in the marketplace. Look for statements such as, "For microwave cooking only" or "Suitable for conventional or microwave cooking" in manufacturers' brochures.
Most microwave safe plastic dishes are suitable for cooking vegetables, meat, poultry, fish and baked goods. Some plastic dishes should not be used for cooking foods with a high fat or sugar content. Check manufacturers' care instructions for recommended cooking uses. Plastic food storage containers can become soft, pitted or distorted from microwave cooking and should not be used. Melamine plastic dishes are not microwave safe.

Cooking Bags designed to withstand boiling, freezing, or conventional heating are microwave safe. Prepare bags according to manufacturer's directions. Close cooking bag with nylon tie provided, otherwise, use a piece of cotton string, or a strip cut from the open end of the bag. Make six ½-inch slits in the top of bag to allow steam to escape. DO NOT use wire twist-tie to close bag. It can act as an antenna and cause arcing (blue sparks). A wire twist-tie could ignite and damage the oven.
DO NOT COOK IN PLASTIC FOOD STORAGE BAGS. They are not heat resistant and may melt.

Plastic Wrap such as SARAN WRAP™ can be used to cover dishes in most recipes. Over an extended cooking time, some disfiguration of the wrap may occur. When removing plastic wrap "covers", as well as any lid, be careful to remove it away from you to avoid steam burns. After cooking, loosen plastic but let dish stand covered.

Paper, Napkins, Wax Paper, Paper Towels, Plates, Cups, and Freezer Wrap

All are handy utensils for microwave cooking. Use them for foods with short cooking times and low fat content. Avoid wax coated paper goods, since the wax may melt onto the food when the food reaches high temperatures. Wax paper is suitable to use to prevent spatter. Disposable polyester coated paperboard pans are sturdy, come in a variety of sizes, and are ideal for microwaving.

CAUTION: DO NOT use recycled paper products, such as brown paper bags, since they contain impurities which may cause arcing (blue sparks) and damage the oven.

Straw, Wicker and Wood

Straw and wicker baskets may be used in the microwave oven for short periods of time to warm rolls or bread. Large wooden utensils, such as bowls or cutting boards should NOT be used for prolonged heating as the microwave energy will cause the wood to become dry and brittle.

Metal

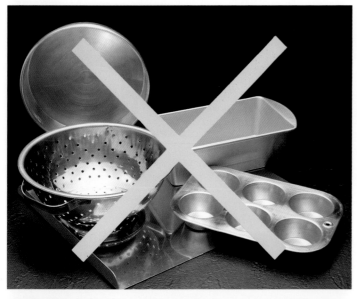

Metal containers or utensils, and those with metallic trim, should NOT be used in the microwave oven. Since microwave energy is reflected by metal, foods in metal containers will not cook evenly.

There is also the possibility of "arcing". This is a static discharge or blue spark between gaps in the metal or between the metal and the interior of the oven. Arcing may cause damage to the oven walls. If arcing occurs, turn the unit off and transfer food to a different container.

Although metal utensils must be avoided in microwave cooking, some metal can be helpful when used correctly.

Aluminum Foil can be used safely if certain guidelines are followed. Because it reflects microwave energy, foil can be used to an advantage in some recipes. It can be used to prevent overcooking. Small pieces of foil are used to cover areas such as chicken wings, tips of roasts, or other thin parts that cook before the rest of the recipe is finished. Foil is used in these cases to slow or stop the cooking process and prevent overcooking.

Foil Lined Containers, either cardboard or plastic, should NOT be used in the microwave oven. Foil lined milk cartons, frozen orange juice concentrate containers, or baking containers included in some cake mixes are examples of things to be avoided.

Frozen Dinner Trays can be used in the microwave oven, but results are satisfactory only if the container is no higher than ¾-inch. In metal containers, all the heating takes place from the top; the metal container reflects the energy directed to the sides and bottom. See Heating Convenience Foods, page 38.

Metal Skewers can be used if there is a large amount of food in proportion to the amount of metal. Take care in the placement of the skewers to avoid arcing between the skewers or between the skewers and the sides of the oven. Wooden skewers are the best and can be easily purchased at your local grocery store, or in the housewares section of many department stores.

Thermometers are available for use in microwave ovens. DO NOT USE CONVENTIONAL MERCURY TYPE CANDY OR MEAT THERMOMETERS in food while heating in the microwave oven.

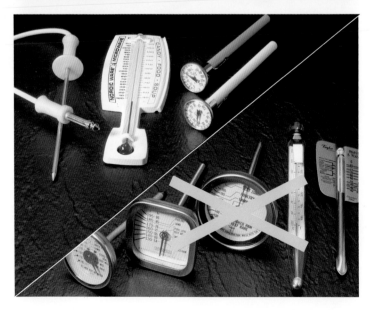

Metal Twist-Ties either paper or plastic coated, should NOT be used in the microwave oven. See pictures and information under COOKING BAGS page 6.

RECIPE PREPARATION and TECHNIQUES

There are few basic rules to be remembered when preparing recipes from this cookbook: All ingredients are taken from their common storage place. Milk, meat, eggs and butter are refrigerator temperature. Canned goods are room temperature. Recipes using canned ingredients include the liquid unless recipe specifies DRAINED. Other facts to remember:

- **Flour** is all-purpose unless another type such as whole wheat is specified.
- **Milk** is homogenized whole milk.
- **Sugar** is granulated white sugar.
- **Brown Sugar** may be light or dark, but should be measured packed.

- **Eggs** are Grade A large.
- **Amounts** given are in standard level measures, i.e., cup, teaspoon, tablespoon.

Food Characteristics

Food characteristics which affect conventional cooking are more pronounced with microwave heating.

Size and Quantity—
Small portions cook faster than large ones.

Shape—Uniform sizes heat more evenly. To compensate for irregular shapes, place thin pieces toward the center of the dish and thicker pieces toward the edge of dish.

Bone and Fat—Both affect heating. Bones may cause irregular cooking. Large amounts of fat absorb microwave energy and meat next to these areas may overcook.

Starting Temperatures—Room temperature foods take less time to cook than refrigerated or frozen foods.

Density—Porous, airy foods take less time to cook than heavy, compact foods.

Browning

Meats and poultry, cooked 10 to 15 minutes, brown from their own fat. Foods cooked for shorter periods of time can be aided with the help of a browning sauce, Worcestershire sauce, or soy sauce. Simply brush one of these sauces over meat or poultry before cooking. Baked goods do not need long cooking time and, therefore, do not brown. When cakes or cupcakes will be frosted, no one will notice this visual difference. For quick breads or muffins, brown sugar can be used in the recipe in place of a portion of granulated sugar, or the surface can be sprinkled with dark spices before baking.

Covering

As with conventional cooking, moisture evaporates during microwave cooking. Because in microwave cooking there is no direct heat, the rate of evaporation cannot be easily controlled. This, however, can be corrected by using different materials to cover dishes. Casserole lids or plastic wrap are used for a tighter seal. Various degrees of less moisture retention can also be obtained by using wax paper or paper towels. However, unless specified, a recipe is cooked uncovered.

When using plastic wrap for a cover for cooking, it is best to leave an area around the edge of the dish to allow steam to escape. However, for Insta-Matic cooking always follow special directions for use of plastic wrap.

Spacing

Individual foods, such as baked potatoes, cupcakes and appetizers, will cook more evenly if placed in the oven equal distance apart. When possible, arrange foods in a circular pattern.

Similarly, when placing foods in a baking dish, arrange around the outside of dish, not lined up next to each other. Food should NOT be stacked on top of each other.

Piercing

The skin or membranes on some foods will cause steam to build up during microwave cooking and the food may burst. Foods must be pierced, scored or have a strip of skin peeled off before cooking to allow steam to escape.

Eggs—Pierce egg yolk twice and egg white several times with a toothpick.

Whole Clams and Oysters—Pierce several times with a toothpick.

Whole Potatoes and Vegetables—Pierce once with a fork.

Apples —Whole apples or new potatoes should have a 1-inch strip of skin peeled off before cooking.

Frankfurters and Sausages—Score smoked sausage and frankfurters. Pierce fresh sausage or brown and serve sausage with a fork.

13

Timing

A range in cooking time is given in each recipe. The time range compensates for the uncontrollable differences in food shapes, starting temperature and regional preferences. Always cook food for the minimum cooking time given in the recipe and check for doneness. If the food is undercooked, continue cooking. It is easier to add time to an undercooked product. Once the food is overcooked, nothing can be done.

Stirring

Stirring is usually necessary during microwave cooking. We have noted when stirring is helpful, using the words once, twice, frequently or occasionally to describe the amount of stirring necessary. Always bring the cooked outside edges toward the center and the less cooked center portions toward the outside.

Turning and Rearranging

It is not possible to stir some foods to redistribute the heat. At times, microwave energy will concentrate in one area of a food. To help insure even cooking, these foods need to be turned or rearranged. Turn over large foods, such as roasts or turkeys, halfway through cooking.

Rearrange small items such as chicken pieces, shrimp, hamburger patties or pork chops. Rearrange pieces from the edge to the center and pieces from the center to the edge of the dish.

In this cookbook there are directions to rotate dishes ½ and ¼ turn. A ½ turn means the back of the dish becomes the front. A ¼ turn means the front and back of the dish becomes the sides.
Rotate, turn and rearrange food according to directions to insure best results.

Standing Time

Most foods will continue to cook by conduction after the microwave oven is turned off. In meat cookery, the internal temperature will rise 5°F to 15°F if allowed to stand, covered, for 10 to 15 minutes. Casseroles and vegetables need a shorter amount of standing time, but this standing time is necessary to allow foods to complete cooking in the center without overcooking on the edges.

Testing for Doneness

The same tests for doneness used in conventional cooking may be used for microwave cooking.

Cakes are done when toothpick comes out clean and cake pulls away from side of the pan.

Chicken is done when juices are clear yellow and drumstick moves freely.

Meat is done when fork-tender or splits at fibers.

Fish is done when it flakes and is opaque.

15

Converting Favorite Recipes

Select recipes that convert easily to microwave cooking such as casseroles, stews, baked chicken, fish and vegetable dishes. The results from foods such as broiled meats, cooked souffles or two-crust pies would be unsatisfactory. Never attempt to deep fat fry in your microwave oven.

A basic rule, when converting conventional recipes to microwave recipes, is to cut the suggested cooking time to one-fourth. Also, find a similar microwave recipe and adapt that time and power setting. Season meats with herbs and spices before cooking; salt after cooking.

Stew meat are not browned before cooking. Omit any oil or fat that would be used for browning. Cut stew meat into 1½-inch pieces. Cut carrots, potatoes and other firm vegetables into small, uniform pieces. Carrots should be thinly sliced and potatoes cut into sixteenths. Reduce liquid by one-fourth. Cover with lid. Cook at HIGH to bring liquid to a boil, cook at LOW until tender. Stir occasionally.

Casseroles microwave cook well. Cut foods into uniform pieces. Condensed soup makes a good base for casseroles. Select a dish that is large enough to allow for stirring. Cooking covered with a lid or plastic wrap reduces cooking time. Stir occasionally during cooking. To keep crumb toppings crisp sprinkle on before stand time.

SPECIAL FEATURES

The information in this section describes the special cooking features available on Quasar microwave ovens. For each feature there is an explanation of how the feature works, how to use the feature and cooking charts for the feature.

The microwave oven you own will not be equipped with every feature. Refer to the oven control panel or operating manual to identify the features on your microwave oven.

The Insta-Matic Cook and Insta-Matic Frozen Foods settings work by detecting a build-up of steam on the humidity sensor. As foods cook in a microwave oven, steam is produced. When foods are covered, the steam will build up and escape from the dish in a burst. This burst of steam is detected by the humidity sensor and the oven automatically calculates the remaining cooking time.

When an Insta-Matic setting is selected the setting number will appear in the display window. The oven door should not be opened for longer than one minute when the setting number appears in the display window.
Opening the door when the setting number is in the display window may cause inaccurate cooking results. Once the steam is detected by the humidity sensor, the remaining cooking time appears in the display window and begins to count-down. At this time, the oven door may be opened, to stir, turn or add foods.

Look for the symbol **I-M** to indicate recipes and charts with Insta-Matic directions. Use these recipes and charts as a basis for determining which of your own similar conventional recipes may be converted to Insta-Matic Cooking.

INSTA-MATIC FROZEN FOODS

The three Insta-Matic Frozen Foods settings are complete cooking cycles which will heat frozen convenience foods to serving temperature. This feature is ideal for heating frozen dinners, casseroles, vegetables, leftovers, hamburgers, and chops.

To select a Frozen Foods setting simply press the Frozen Foods control until the desired setting number is reached. Refer to the sections "Preparing Food For Cooking On Insta-Matic Frozen Foods" on page 22. for information on freezing and heating hamburgers, chops, casseroles and leftovers. Refer to the section "Heating Frozen Convenience Foods On Insta-Matic" on page 39 for information on heating Frozen dinners and breakfasts.

Listed below are the recommended foods and their appropriate Frozen Foods setting.

INSTA-MATIC FROZEN FOODS	
1	Casseroles/Frozen Dinners
2	Vegetables/Side Dishes
3	Hamburgers/Chops

COOK and FROZEN FOODS

INSTA-MATIC COOK

The eight Insta-Matic Cook settings are designed for use with many types of foods fresh, canned foods, package goods and refrigerated items. All foods should be taken from their normal storage places. For example, meat, poultry, fish and dairy products should be at refrigerator temperature, while canned goods and cake mixes should be at room temperature.

To select a COOK setting simply press the COOK control until the desired setting number is reached. For all settings, except COOK 8, when the steam is sensed by the humidity sensor the remaining cooking time will appear in the display window and count-down. On the COOK 8 setting, cooking is completed when the steam is detected. A cooking time will NOT appear in the display window.

Listed below are some of the recommended foods and their appropriate COOK settings.

INSTA-MATIC COOK	
1	Reheat
2	Meat Loaf/Pot Roast/Round Steak
3	Rice/Lasagna/Sausage
4	Poultry Pieces/Casseroles/Fish
5	Potatoes/Root Vegetables
6	Corn/Peas/Broccoli/Spinach
7	Hamburgers/Shrimp/Meatballs
8	Appetizers/Noodles/Sauces

Consult recipes or charts for special procedures.

CUSTOM COOK

The Custom Cook control is designed to be used in conjunction with any of the Insta-Matic Frozen Foods or Insta-Matic Cook settings. For example, after cooking vegetables or any other food for the first time, with your new microwave oven, you may find that the food is not cooked exactly to your liking, Custom Cook is the answer. The next time you cook that specific food, or one similar, choose the correct Insta-Matic setting and then simply press the Custom Cook control once to cook food a little more or twice to cook slightly less... press the Start control and the oven is programmed to cook the food to your personal taste.

Insta-Matic Cooking Hints

For proper cooking results on the Insta-Matic settings, the directions given in the recipes and charts for container size and coverings must be followed. Lids should fit properly and be the one designed for the container.

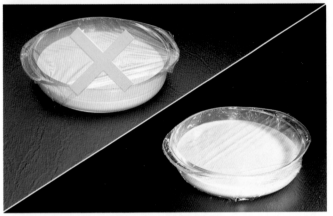

Cover dishes without matching lids COMPLETELY with plastic wrap. Securely mold wrap around sides of dish. Steam builds up under plastic wrap and lids; remove them away from you to avoid steam burns.

Do not open oven door longer than one minute when Insta-Matic setting number is in display window. Cooking results may be unsuccessful. Open the door during the second stage of cooking (i.e. when cooking time appears and counts down) to turn over pot roasts, or stir, glaze or shield foods as recipe or chart directs.

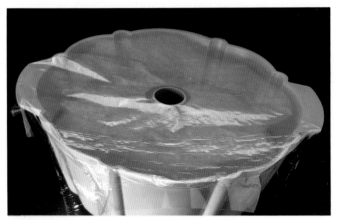

Do not use nonglossy plastic microwave safe cookware. Plastic wrap does not adhere tightly to nonglossy plastic dishes. Plastic wrap also may not adhere to some glass cookware with large decorative coatings on the outside of the dish.

Loosen or remove plastic wrap as recipe directs for stand time.

Reheating Food
(Refrigerated or Room Temperature)

Below are guidelines to follow when reheating various types of foods. Foods are heated covered on Insta-Matic Cook 1.

Plates of food—Arrange food on plate; top with butter, gravy, etc. Loosely, but completely cover plate with plastic wrap. Heat on Insta-Matic Cook 1. After Insta-Matic heating, release plastic wrap. Let stand, covered, 2 minutes before serving.

Canned foods—Empty contents into casserole dish or serving bowl; cover dish with casserole lid or plastic wrap. Heat on Insta-Matic Cook 1. After Insta-Matic heating, release plastic wrap. Let stand, covered, 2 minutes before serving.

Casseroles—Make sure container is dry on the outside and free from all moisture. Add 2 to 4 tablespoons liquid; cover with lid or plastic wrap. Heat on Insta-Matic Cook 1. Let stand 2 to 3 minutes before serving.

Note: *Only the foods listed above are suitable for reheating with the Insta-Matic Cook setting. To reheat other foods refer to pages 36–42.*

General Care Information for Temperature Probes

Insert the Temperature probe at least one inch into the food to insure an accurate temperature reading.

Do NOT use the probe with frozen foods or a browning dish.

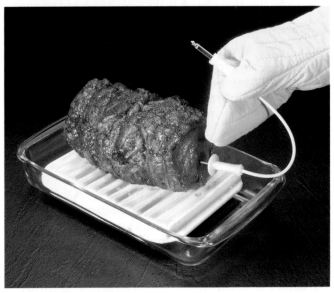

Remove probe from oven cavity receptacle with a pot holder.

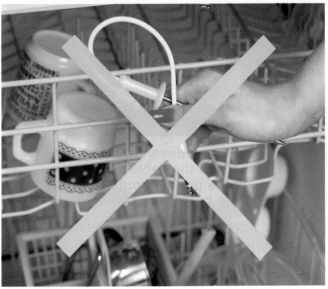

Clean probe with mild detergent and a soft cloth. Do NOT immerse in water or wash in the dishwasher. Store in its original container.

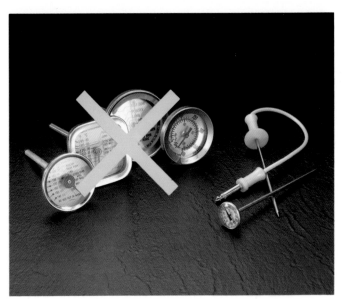

DO NOT USE A CONVENTIONAL MEAT THERMOMETER IN FOOD WHILE COOKING IN THE MICROWAVE OVEN. A conventional meat thermometer may be used to check the internal temperature of a food item. A microwave safe thermometer may be used during cooking.

DEFROSTING

Defrosting frozen foods is one of the benefits of having a
microwave oven. To achieve the best results, follow our
recommended techniques for freezing and defrosting.

Preparing Meat for Freezing

The finished quality of the prepared food will depend on the original quality before freezing, the care the food receives during freezing, and the techniques and times used for defrosting. Select good quality, fresh meat, poultry, or fish for freezing. Foods should be frozen as soon as possible after purchasing to preserve their quality. How foods are wrapped for freezing and the temperature they are frozen at, affect defrosting results. Proper wrapping materials and packaging techniques should be used for best results.

WRAPPING MATERIALS best suited for use in the freezer are odorless, and moisture and vapor proof. Meats need to be removed from their wrappings before defrosting. Therefore, containers such as glass freezer jars and plastic freezer containers are unsuitable. Heavy-duty plastic wraps and bags, and freezer wrap are suitable. If aluminum foil is used for wrapping, all pieces of foil should be removed before defrosting in your microwave oven. Otherwise, arcing may occur. Meats may also be frozen in their store packaging for short periods of time.

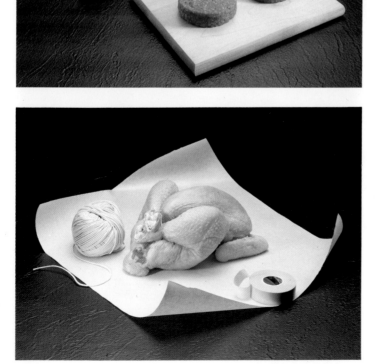

When WRAPPING FOR FREEZING, arrange meat in thin, uniform layers. Package ground meat in 1 to 2-inch thick rectangular, square or round shapes. Chicken pieces, chops and stew meat will defrost more easily if frozen in 1 or 2 piece layers rather than in bulky, thick packages. To aid in separating chops and hamburger patties during defrosting, place two pieces of wax paper between the layers.

REMOVE GIBLETS from fresh whole poultry. (The giblets may be frozen separately, if desired.) Clean and dry poultry. Tie legs and wings with string; this helps poultry keep its shape during freezing. If poultry is packaged frozen, it may be defrosted even though the giblets are inside the cavity. However, the cavity will be very icy after the defrosting cycle. It will be necessary to run cold water over the poultry.

FISH AND SEAFOODS are best frozen in single layers. Fillets may be frozen 2 or 3 deep, but place two pieces of wax paper or plastic wrap between each layer. Shrimp or scallops may be quick frozen on a cookie sheet covered with plastic wrap. Once they are frozen, simply remove from the cookie sheet and place in a freezer bag or container. If they are thoroughly frozen before placing in the bag, they will not stick to each other.

REMOVE ALL AIR before sealing plastic bags. The drug store wrap is a good wrapping procedure to follow when using sheets of wrap such as freezer or plastic wrap. Center food to be wrapped on material. Bring two edges, up over the center and start folding down in 1 inch tucks until wrap is close to meat. Remove excess air from package. Shape ends into triangles and fold up over center. Tape securely. Label package with type and cut of meat, date and weight.

FREEZE FOODS in a freezer which is maintained at 0°F or lower. Defrosting times given in the charts are for completely frozen foods.

DEFROSTING CONTROLS
WEIGHT DEFROST

Weight Defrost can be used to defrost many cuts of meat, poultry and fish by weight. To use, simply program the weight of the food in pounds (1.0) and tenths of a pound (0.1). The oven can be programmed from 0.1 pound (approximately 1½ ounces) to 8.0 pounds.

Once the oven is programmed it will determine the defrosting time and power levels. The defrosting time will appear in the display window after the Start Control is touched.

Listed below are the recommended foods that can be defrosted on Weight Defrost.

BEEF	Roasts, ribs, stew meat, steaks, ground beef, liver
PORK	Roast, chops, ground pork, frankfurters
LAMB	Roast, chops, ground lamb
POULTRY	Whole or split cornish hens, Whole or cut up chicken, Whole Turkey or Turkey parts
FISH	Individual fillets, steaks
SEAFOOD	Shrimp (medium), sea scallops

Before using Weight Defrost make sure the meat, poultry or fish has been properly frozen. See, "Preparing Meats for Freezing" on page 26. For best results follow Defrosting Directions. Foods that are not recommended for Weight Defrost can be defrosted using Multi-Stage Time Defrost. Follow the times and information given in the Multi-Stage Time Defrosting section.

DEFROSTING DIRECTIONS FOR WEIGHT DEFROST

BEFORE STARTING

CONVERT ounces to tenths of a pound. Meats packaged in most grocery stores are labeled with the weight in pound and hundredths of a pound. See conversion chart below.

Conversion Chart
Follow this chart to convert ounces or hundredths of a pound into tenths of a pound.

Ounces	Hundredths of a Pound	Tenths of a Pound
0	.01–.05	0.0
1–2	.06–.15	0.1
3–4	.16–.25	0.2
5	.26–.35	0.3
6–7	.36–.45	0.4
8	.46–.55	0.5
9–10	.56–.65	0.6
11–12	.66–.75	0.7
13	.76–.85	0.8
14–15	.86–.95	0.9
16	.96–.99	0.0

Examples: *If a roast weighs 5.95 pounds or 5 pounds 14 ounces, program 5.9 pounds. If a roast weighs 5.99 pounds or 6 pounds 0 ounces, program 6.0 pounds.*

REMOVE WRAPPER. Otherwise, the wrap will hold steam and juice close to the food which can cause the outer surface of the food to cook.

REMOVE ground meat from its TRAY. Place meat in an appropriate size dish.

PLACE ROAST FAT-SIDE DOWN and WHOLE POULTRY BREAST-SIDE DOWN on a microwave roasting rack in an oblong dish. The rack helps prevent the food from sitting in its own juice. The juice will get hot during defrosting and if the food is sitting in the juice, the bottom will begin to cook.

PLACE SMALL ITEMS, such as chops, chicken pieces, shrimp, scallops, fish on a microwave roasting rack in an oblong dish.

29

AT THE FIRST BEEP

TURN OVER beef and pork roasts, ground meat, whole poultry, stew meat, shrimp, or scallops.
BREAK APART chops, poultry pieces, shrimp or scallops.
REMOVE defrosted portion from ground meat, stew meat, shrimp or scallops.

AT THE SECOND BEEP

TURN OVER ground meat, stew meat, whole chickens, whole fish or fillets.
BREAK APART stew meat, ground meat, poultry pieces, shrimp or scallops.
SEPARATE chops, hamburger patties, and fillets.
REMOVE defrosted ground meat, stew meat, poultry pieces, shrimp or scallops.
SHIELD ends of roast, fat or bones with foil.

AFTER DEFROSTING

LARGE ROASTS may still be icy in center. Allow to stand in the refrigerator to finish defrosting.

WHOLE POULTRY may still be icy in center. Run cold water in cavity. If poultry was frozen with giblets in the cavity, after defrosting run cold water in the cavity until the giblets can be removed.

SMALL ITEMS such as chops, steaks, cornish hens, or shrimp can stand 10 to 15 minutes. Use this time to prepare the remaining ingredients for cooking.

MULTI-STAGE TIME DEFROST

To use Multi-Stage Time Defrost, touch the DEFROST pad and program the defrosting time. The oven will divide the defrost time into eight stages: 4 defrost and 4 stand periods. During the programmed time, the oven will alternate between defrost power and stand times (no power). Follow Defrosting times and directions given in this section.

DEFROSTING MEATS

Meat should be frozen in moisture and vapor proof wrapping materials. Small items such as chops, hamburger patties, etc. should be frozen in 1 or 2 piece layers.

Remove meat from original wrapper and set on a microwave roasting rack placed in oblong dish. Set DEFROST and the time recommended in the chart.

Turn meat over two or three times during defrost cycle. Shield edges and unevenly shaped ends of roasts halfway through the defrost cycle.

Halfway through the defrost cycle break apart ground beef, separate chops and remove meat that is defrosted.

Large roasts may still be icy in center. Allow to stand.

MEAT	DEFROST TIME (minutes per pound)
BEEF	
ROASTS	
Tenderloin	10 to 12
Chuck or rump	10 to 12
Sirloin, rolled	10 to 12
STEAK	
Boneless sirloin	12 to 14
Flank	8 to 10
MISCELLANEOUS	
Frankfurters	10 to 12
Ground beef	10 to 12
Liver	10 to 12
PORK	
ROASTS	12 to 14
RIBS	12 to 14
CHOPS	12 to 14
Estimated times for meats not listed above.	10 to 12

DEFROSTING POULTRY AND GAME

Poultry and game should be frozen in moisture and vapor proof wrapping materials. For best results cut-up chicken should be frozen in a single layer. Remove poultry or game from original wrapper and set on a microwave roasting rack placed in an 12×8-inch dish.

Set Defrost and the time recommended in the chart. Turn poultry or game over two to four times during defrosting. Halfway through the defrost cycle shield end of drumsticks, wings and breast bones. Also, break apart cut-up chickens and remove small pieces such as wings, that may defrost before larger pieces.

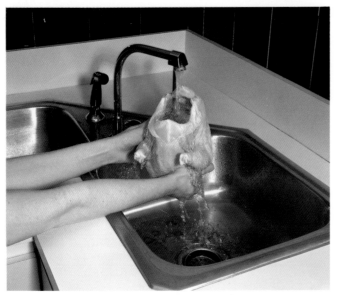

Rinse poultry or game under cold water to remove ice crystals.

POULTRY	DEFROST TIME (minutes per pound)
CHICKEN	
Whole	12 to 14
Cut-up	8 to 10
Boneless breasts	12 to 14
CORNISH HENS, WHOLE	12 to 16
DUCK, WHOLE	16 to 18
GOOSE, WHOLE	10 to 12
PHEASANT, WHOLE	16 to 18
TURKEY	
Whole	12 to 14
Half	16 to 18
Estimated times for poultry not listed above.	10 to 12

DEFROSTING FISH AND SEAFOOD

Fish and seafood should be frozen in moisture and vapor proof wrapping materials. Small items such as scallops or shrimp should be frozen in a single layer. Remove fish from original wrapper and set on microwave roasting rack placed in a 12×8-inch dish.

Set Defrost and the time recommended in chart. Halfway through the defrost cycle, turn whole fish or blocks of fillets over. Also, break apart shrimp or scallops. Remove any pieces that are defrosted.

FISH	DEFROST TIME (minutes per pound)
Crabmeat	30 to 32
Fish Fillets	8 to 12
Fish Steaks	10 to 12
Lobster Tails	12 to 14
Sea Scallops	16 to 20
Shrimp, medium	12 to 14
Whole Fish	10 to 12
Estimated times for fish and seafood not listed above.	12 to 14

DEFROSTING FROZEN CONVENIENCE FOODS

Food that normally takes several hours at room temperature to defrost, can be defrosted in the microwave oven. Cakes, rolls, and frozen fruits and vegetables are defrosted in a matter of minutes. Consult Chart for recommended defrosting times and techniques.

Remove layer cake from original container. Place on a microwave safe dish. Defrost according to time given in chart. Center will be slightly icy after defrost time. Allow to stand at room temperature.

Wrap roll or danish in paper towel. Defrost according to time given in chart.

Defrost frozen whipped topping in original plastic tub for time given in chart.

DEFROSTING FROZEN CONVENIENCE FOODS

ITEM	POWER	DEFROST TIME (in minutes)	SPECIAL HINTS
BAKED GOODS	DEFROST		Remove from original container; arrange on serving plate.
Brownies (13 oz.)		4 to 6	
Cupcakes (6) (10 to 11 oz.)		3 to 5	Add an additional 1 to 1½ minutes to serve warm.
Cheese Cake (17 oz.)		7 to 9	
Layer Cakes (17 to 18 oz.)		3 to 5	
Pound Cake (10¾ oz.)		2 to 4	
Coffee Cake (11 to 12 oz.)		6 to 8	
BAGELS	DEFROST		
2		4 to 6	
4		6 to 8	
DANISH	DEFROST		Each individually wrapped in a paper towel (for 1 or 2).
1		1 to 2	
2		3 to 4	Arrange on paper plate; cover with paper towel (for 4 to 6).
4 (9 oz. package)		5 to 7½	
6 (13 oz. package)		7 to 9½	
Dinner Rolls (6)	DEFROST	3 to 5	
Donuts	DEFROST		
Plain or Sugar coated			
1		1½ to 2	
2		2 to 3	
4		5 to 6	
6		8 to 9	
Hard Rolls (1 to 1¼ oz. ea.)	DEFROST		
1		1 to 1½	
2		2 to 3	
4		4 to 5	
MISCELLANEOUS (TO THAW)			
Frozen Juice Concentrates	MEDIUM		Remove lid. If container is foil lined, remove to pitcher.
(6 oz.)		1½ to 2½	
(12 oz.)		3 to 5	
Non-Dairy Creamer (16 oz.)	DEFROST	18 to 20	Open carton. Shake vigerously 2 times during defrosting. Defrost in original plastic tub.
Pancake/Muffin Batter (10 oz.)	DEFROST	8 to 10	
Whipped Topping (9 oz.)	DEFROST	4 to 6	
Frozen Mixed Fruit (10 oz.)	DEFROST	9 to 11	Pierce pouch or remove metal lid; set on saucer.
Frozen Vegetables	DEFROST		Remove from box. Break apart after 3 minutes. If vegetables are in a pouch, pierce pouch.
(6 oz.)		6 to 8	
(10 oz.)		10 to 12	

CONVENIENCE FOODS

Quick and easy reheating of frozen foods, is one of the many benefits of microwave oven. Many frozen convenience foods are heated in less time than it would take in a conventional oven. The Frozen Convenience Food chart gives suggested power levels, cooking times and techniques for successful reheating results. In addition, check manufacturer's heating directions. Many convenience foods now include microwave directions.

FROZEN CONVENIENCE FOODS

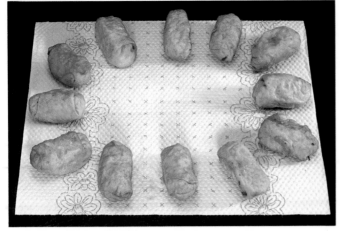

Place bite-size appetizers on a paper towel lined paper plate. Arrange 12 appetizers in a circular pattern.

Frozen dinners may be heated in the foil tray, if the tray is less than ¾-inch high.

Frozen dinners and breakfasts are now available in paperboard and microwave safe plastic tray. These dinners may be heated directly in the tray.

If there is a foil cover, remove it from the tray. Some foods such as breads, french fries, or cake like desserts such as brownies do not microwave well. These can be removed from the tray.

Cover the tray with plastic wrap, or use plastic lid or film which accompanies some dinners. Vent lids according to manufacturers directions.

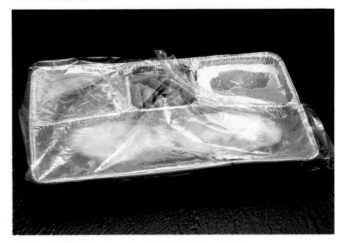

When using plastic wrap do not cover desserts. Desserts cook better uncovered. Cook cake like desserts in a custard cup 1½ to 2½ minutes at HIGH.

HEATING CANNED GOODS

Empty contents of can into serving dish or casserole.

Choose a casserole large enough to allow for stirring.

Food spread out in a shallow dish will heat more quickly than the same food heated in a narrow deep dish.

Cover with a lid or plastic wrap. Stir occasionally during heating.

Let stand, covered, 3 minutes before serving.

Food	Approx. Cooking Time (in minutes) at MEDIUM-HIGH
Chili (15 oz.)	3½ to 4½
Corned Beef Hash (15½ oz.)	3 to 4
Gravy (10½ oz.)	2 to 3½
Pork and Beans 16 oz. 20¾ oz.	 3½ to 4½ 5 to 6
Soup 10¾ oz. plus 1 can liquid 20 oz.	 4 to 5 4 to 5
Spaghetti 7¾ oz. 14 to 19 oz.	 3 to 4 5 to 6
Spaghetti Sauce 15½ oz. 32 oz.	 3½ to 5 8 to 10
Vegetables 8 oz. 16 to 17 oz.	 2 to 3 3 to 4

Reheating Leftovers

The microwave oven is ideal for reheating leftovers. Most leftovers will reach serving temperature in a matter of minutes and will taste freshly cooked. Follow our guidelines listed below to prepare foods for reheating. Always use microwave safe plates and dishes. If there is any doubt if a dish is microwave safe, perform the dish test given on page 5.

The times given in the reheating chart are for foods that are refrigerator temperature.

Meats

Sliced meat will heat more evenly and quickly than a roast, and thin slices more quickly than thick slices. Arrange slices flat on a plate. Cover with wax paper. Sauce or gravy may be poured over meat before reheating to help keep meat moist.

To reheat chops, arrange on a dish with the thicker portion toward the edge of the dish. Cover with wax paper.

Casseroles

For quick heating, spread out individual servings in a single serving casserole. Cover with lid or plastic wrap. For several servings, heat in a 1½-quart casserole. If necessary, stir in a small amount of liquid (water, milk, gravy or broth). Cover with a lid or plastic wrap. Casseroles with crumb toppings should be covered with wax paper. This will help prevent the crumb topping from becoming soggy. Stir casseroles several times during heating. Casseroles, such as lasagna which cannot be stirred, should be rotated ¼ turn twice during heating.

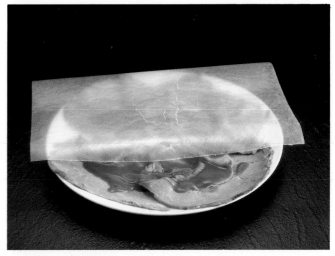

Plates of food

Arrange food on the plate with the thicker, denser food along the edge of the plate. Food that reheats quickly such as vegetables should be placed in the middle of the plate. However, mashed potatoes which are dense, should be spread out along the edge for quicker heating. Cover with wax paper or plastic wrap. Rotate plate ¼ turn halfway through heating.

Pastries

Place pastry on a paper plate. Heat 10 to 40 seconds. The filling and glazes will be hotter than the pastry. Be careful when eating.

Slice of Pie

Place slice of pie on plate. Heat 1 to 1½ minutes.

Rolls

Wrap individual roll in paper towel. Heat 5 to 10 seconds. Arrange 4 to 6 rolls in a serving container. Cover with a paper towel or napkin. Heat 30 seconds. Test baked goods before adding more time; when overheated they become tough and hard.

Vegetables

Reheat covered just until very warm. If possible, stir or rearrange during heating.

Sandwiches

Wrap closed sandwiches in a paper towel and place on glass tray. Place open-faced sandwiches on plate and cover with wax paper. Heat until sandwiches are just warm.

ITEM	APPROX. HEATING TIME (in minutes) at MEDIUM-HIGH	STAND TIME
Casseroles		
Individual serving (about 1 cup)	1½ to 2	1
Small casserole (about 3 cups)	6 to 10	2
Meats		
1 chop (about 5 oz.)	1¼ to 1½	1
2 chops (about 5 oz. ea.)	1¾ to 2	1
½ pound meat, sliced thin	2 to 2½	1
1 pound meat, sliced thin	2¾ to 3	1
½ pound meat, sliced thick	2½ to 3	1
1 pound meat, sliced thick	3 to 3½	1
Pastries		
1 doughnut	¼	1
2 doughnuts	½	1
4 doughnuts	¾ to 1	1
Pie		
1 slice	1 to 1½	1
2 slices	2 to 2½	1
Plate of Food (1)	2¼ to 3	2
Rolls		
2	¼	½
4	½	1
Sandwiches		
Open-faced		
1	1½ to 1¾	1
2	2 to 2¼	1
Closed		
1	1¼ to 1½	1
2	1¾ to 2¼	1
Vegetables		
1 cup	1 to 1½	1
3 cups	4 to 5	2

CANNING
DO NOT USE YOUR MICROWAVE
OVEN FOR CANNING

Canning and sterilizing of canning jars should NOT be done in a microwave oven. Home canning destroys mold, yeast, bacteria and enzymes in foods to prevent spoilage.

Low acid and nonacid foods require a temperature of 240°F, which is above the boiling point of water. In canning 240°F, is obtained by using a pressure canner set at 10 pounds pressure (at sea level). Your microwave oven can only bring plain water to the boiling points. (212°F).

High acid foods are processed in a hot water bath canner. The canning jars are covered with water which is kept at a rolling boil. Your microwave oven cannot duplicate this procedure. Since canning jars also need to be submerged in water for sterilization, it would be impossible to do this procedure in a microwave oven.

In addition, certain canning lids and rings may cause arcing in the microwave oven.

Improperly canned food may spoil. If spoiled food is consumed it can cause illness or death. We recommend that canning be done only on a conventional range top following standard canning procedures.

QUASAR RECOMMENDS THE
FOLLOWING REGARDING COOKING
IN YOUR MICROWAVE OVEN:

1. Small quantities of food or foods with low moisture content can burn, dry out or catch on fire if cooked too long. If a fire occurs, turn the oven off and leave the oven door closed. Disconnect the power cord, or shut off power at the fuse box or circuit breaker panel.

2. Regular popcorn must be popped only in a microwave corn popper. Many brands are available through local retail stores. In addition, special microwave popcorn is available in some areas of the country. This popcorn pops in its own package and does not require a microwave corn popper. It may be used in this oven.

3. Do not attempt to deep fat fry in your oven.

4. Dry only herbs in your microwave oven. Follow directions given in this cookbook and do not leave oven unattended.

5. Do not use paper towels which contain a synthetic fiber woven into them, such as nylon. Synthetic fibers may cause the towel to ignite.

6. Do not use the oven for any reason other than the preparation of food or specific uses indicated in this cookbook.

PRECAUTIONS TO AVOID POSSIBLE EXPOSURE TO EXCESSIVE MICROWAVE ENERGY

(a) **Do not attempt to operate this oven with the door open** since open-door operation can result in harmful exposure to microwave energy. It is important not to defeat or tamper with the safety interlocks.

(b) **Do not place any object** between the oven front face and the door or allow soil or cleaner residue to accumulate on sealing surfaces.

(c) **Do not operate the oven** if it is damaged. It is particularly important that the oven door close properly and that there is no damage to the :
   (1) door (bent)
   (2) hinges and latches (broken or loosened)
   (3) door seals and sealing surfaces

(d) **The oven should not be adjusted or repaired** by anyone except properly qualified service personnel.

BEFORE CALLING FOR SERVICE

Many times a service call can be avoided by checking a few simple things. The following conditions are not caused by a defect in the unit itself, so please check the following points before requesting service.

Condition	Time-Saving Checks
No Power	★Oven plugged in? ★Check home fuse or circuit breaker.
Oven not operating	★Oven door closed? ★Controls set properly?
Takes longer than time in cookbook	★Incorrect power selection? ★Low voltage at power outlet? ★Starting temperature and shape of foods vary, so simply cook a little longer.
Uneven cooking Undercooking or Overcooking	★Improperly wrapped or used incorrect container? ★Controls set properly? ★For large cuts of meat, utilize standing time at room temperature after cooking.
Oven light flickers	★This is normal.
Water condensation around door	★This is normal—merely wipe dry.
Arcing occurs	★Metallic wrap or container touching oven wall. ★Dish or glassware trimmed in gold or silver. ★Container has metal parts or trim.

OVEN MEALS

Total oven meals can be prepared in your microwave oven. Plan the order of the meal so that the foods that have the longest cooking and stand time are prepared first. The foods that need to be served immediately should be prepared last. Desserts can be prepared first and allowed to chill or stand, covered, or they can be prepared during the meal and served warm. At times it may be necessary to reheat a food for 1 or 2 minutes just before serving. To get you started, we have included Step-by-Step instructions for an easily prepared breakfast, lunch and dinner.

BREAKFAST

MENU:
Orange Juice
Baked Eggs in Bologna Cups
Raisin Bran Muffins

Prepare Raisin Bran Muffins, page 199.

Keep muffins covered until ready to use.
Prepare recipe for Baked Eggs in Bologna Cups on page 151.

Pour juice while eggs are cooking. Approximate cooking time is 15 minutes.

LUNCH

MENU:
Meat Loaf
Baked Potatoes
Fresh Broccoli
Raisin Bread Pudding
Iced Tea

Prepare Raisin Bread Pudding according to recipe on page 217.

Prepare Midget Meat Loaf according to recipe on page 94.

While meat loaf stands, bake potatoes according to chart on pages 167 and 169.

After cooking wrap potatoes in foil. Prepare broccoli according to chart on pages 166 and 169. Pour iced tea. Approximate cooking time is 45 minutes.

DINNER

MENU:
Apricot Glazed Chicken
Chicken Flavored Rice
(from mix)
Green Beans Amandine
Chilled Chocolate Almond
Souffle

Prepare Chocolate Souffle according to recipe on page 216. Souffle needs to be chilled for at least 3 hours so prepare early in the day.

Prepare rice according to chart on page 188.

Let rice stand, covered, until ready to serve. Meanwhile, prepare Apricot Glazed Chicken recipe on page113. After cooking let stand, covered until ready to serve.

Assemble Green Beans Amandine, while chicken is cooking. Cook while chicken is standing.
If necessary, reheat rice or chicken 2 to 3 minutes while beans are standing.
Approximate cooking time is 1 hour.

APPETIZERS and BEVERAGES

Hot appetizers and beverages take only minutes to heat in a microwave. Assemble and refrigerate appetizers before company arrives. When needed, place appetizers on microwave safe serving dish and heat. Hot appetizers can be easily prepared throughout a party.

CHILI DIP OLÉ

½ **pound ground beef**
1 large onion, finely chopped
1 envelope (1¼ oz.) chili seasoning mix
1 can (6 oz.) tomato paste
1 tablespoon sugar, optional
Corn chips

Yield: 2 Cups

Crumble ground beef in medium glass bowl. Stir in onions. Cook at **HIGH** 3 to 4 minutes, or until beef is browned; stir once. Drain. Stir in chili seasoning, tomato paste and sugar. Cook at **HIGH** 3 to 4 minutes. Serve warm with corn chips.

Crumble ground beef in medium bowl. Stir in onions.

Cook at HIGH 3 to 4 minutes, or until beef is browned. Stir once.

Drain grease from ground beef mixture. Stir in chili seasoning, tomato paste and sugar. Cook at HIGH 3 to 4 minutes.

APPETIZER PÂTÉ I-M

1 pound chicken livers, halved
½ cup chicken broth
1 small onion, chopped
¼ teaspoon thyme
4 slices bacon, cooked (see page 87)
¼ cup butter or margarine, softened (see page 234)
1 tablespoon sherry, optional
½ teaspoon garlic salt
Dash pepper
Parsley flakes

Yield: 1⅓ Cups

In medium glass bowl, combine livers, broth, onion and thyme. Cover completely with plastic wrap.

TO COOK BY INSTA-MATIC: Cook on **COOK 3.** When time appears in display window, stir once.

TO COOK BY TIME: Cook at **HIGH** 2 to 3 minutes and at **MEDIUM** 3 to 4 minutes; stir once.

TO COMPLETE: Drain and reserve ¼ cup liquid. With electric mixer, blender or food processor, puree liver and onion mixture, reserved broth, bacon, butter, sherry, garlic and pepper until smooth. Spoon into crock or small bowl. Sprinkle with parsley and chill. Serve as spread with crackers.

BACON BITES

4 slices bacon, halved
8 frozen potato puffs defrosted (see page 35), canned pineapple chunks or water chestnuts

Yield: 8 Hors d'oeuvres

Place bacon between layers of paper towel on paper plate. Cook at **HIGH** 1½ to 2 minutes, or until partially cooked. Wrap bacon around potato and secure with wooden toothpick. Arrange on paper towel lined paper plate. Cook at **HIGH** 1½ to 2 minutes. Serve immediately.

COCKTAIL MEATBALLS I-M

½ pound ground beef
1 egg, beaten
¼ cup Italian flavored dry bread crumbs
1 clove garlic, finely chopped
2 tablespoons finely chopped green onion
½ teaspoon salt
¼ teaspoon basil leaves, crushed
Dash pepper
½ cup grape jelly
½ cup chili sauce
1 tablespoon prepared mustard

Yield: 24 Meatballs

In medium bowl, combine ground beef egg, bread crumbs, garlic, onion and seasonings. Mix lightly. Shape in 24 bite-size meatballs. In 2-quart casserole, combine jelly, chili sauce and mustard. Mix until well blended. Add meatballs. Cover with lid.

TO COOK BY INSTA-MATIC: Cook on **COOK 7.** After time appears in display window, stir twice.

TO COOK BY TIME: Cook at **HIGH** 6 minutes and **MEDIUM-LOW** 9 minutes. Stir twice.

TO COMPLETE: Stir. Let stand, uncovered, 3 minutes before serving.

NEPTUNE'S CHEESE CANAPES

1 package (10 oz.) sharp Cheddar cold pack cheese food
⅓ cup butter or margarine
1 can (6 oz.) crabmeat, drained and flaked*
1 tablespoon flour
Dash hot pepper sauce
6 English muffins, split and toasted

Yield: 48 Canapes

Combine cheese and butter in medium glass bowl. Cook at **LOW** 1½ to 2 minutes, or until softened. Stir in crab, flour and pepper sauce; spread on muffins. Cut each muffin into quarters and garnish, if desired, with pimento or paprika. Arrange 12 canapes on paper plate or microwave safe serving tray. Cook at **MEDIUM** ½ to 1 minute or until crab mixture begins to melt.
Repeat procedure with remaining ingredients.

***Substitution:** Use 1 can (7 oz.) tuna, drained and flaked.*

51

HOLIDAY CHEESE BALL

1 package (3 oz.) cream cheese, softened
  (see page 234)
3 cups (12 oz.) shredded Cheddar cheese
¼ cup flour
¼ cup white wine
¼ teaspoon onion powder
⅛ teaspoon garlic powder
⅛ teaspoon Worcestershire sauce
⅓ cup finely chopped nuts or parsley
  flakes

Yield: 1 (6 inch) Ball

In medium glass bowl, combine cream
cheese, Cheddar cheese, flour, wine, onion,
garlic and Worcestershire. Cook at **WARM** 5
minutes. With electric mixer, beat until
smooth. Shape into ball and roll in nuts;
chill. Cook at **WARM** 3 minutes, or until
spreadable; serve.

CHEESE AND SPINACH I-M CRUSTLESS QUICHE

4 eggs
⅓ cup half'n half
1½ cups (6 oz.) shredded Swiss cheese
1 package (10 oz.) frozen spinach, cooked
  and drained (see pages 167 and 170)
4 slices bacon, crisp-cooked and crumbled
  (see page 87)
1 teaspoon lemon juice
½ teaspoon salt

Yield: 10 Servings

Beat eggs with half'n half until light and
fluffy. Blend in cheese, spinach, bacon,
lemon juice and salt. Pour into lightly
greased 9-inch quiche dish.

TO COOK BY INSTA-MATIC: Cover
completely with plastic wrap. Cook on
COOK 6.

TO COOK BY TIME: Cook at **MEDIUM** 10 to
12 minutes.

TO COMPLETE: Quiche is done when knife
inserted near center comes out clean. Let
stand, uncovered, 5 minutes. Cut into 10
wedges to serve.

PARTY BLUE CHEESE SPREAD

1 envelope unflavored gelatin
¾ cup water
1 tablespoon lemon juice
1 package (3 oz.) cream cheese, softened
  (see page 234)
⅓ cup milk
¼ pound blue cheese, crumbled
½ cup sour cream
¼ cup diced green pepper or finely
  chopped walnuts
2 teaspoons Worcestershire sauce

Yield: 3 Cups

In small glass bowl, sprinkle unflavored gelatin over water. Heat at **HIGH** 2½ to 3 minutes, or until gelatin is dissolved; stir twice. Add lemon juice; cool slightly. Blend cream cheese and milk until smooth; stir in blue cheese, sour cream, green pepper, Worcestershire and gelatin mixture.
Turn into 3-cup mold or bowl and chill until firm. Unmold and serve with crackers as a spread.

MARINATED VEGETABLE BITES

4 cups cut-up fresh vegetables
  (about ½-in. pieces)
½ cup Italian dressing

Yield: 4 Cups

In 12×8-inch dish, toss vegetables with Italian dressing. Cook, covered with plastic wrap, at **HIGH** 6 to 7 minutes, or until vegetables are crisp-tender; stir once. Chill before serving.

Hint: Choose a variety of vegetables that cook in about the same time (see Vegetable Charts, pages 166, 167 and 169). If using vegetables with different cooking times, cut vegetable with shorter cooking time into larger pieces.

MEXICALE FIESTA DIP

1 pound pasteurized process cheese
  spread, cubed
1 can (16 oz.) whole tomatoes, drained
  and chopped
1 can (4 oz.) green chilies, drained and
  chopped
¼ teaspoon cumin seed
Dash hot pepper sauce
Taco chips

Yield: 3 Cups

In large glass bowl, combine cheese, tomatoes, chilies, cumin seed and hot pepper sauce. Cook at **MEDIUM-LOW** 9 to 10 minutes. Stir occasionally.
Stir; let stand, covered, 3 minutes. Stir before serving. Serve warm with taco chips.

SURPRISE VEGETABLE DIP I-M

1 package (8 oz.) cream cheese
  (cut into 1-inch cubes)
1 jar (5 oz.) pasteurized process cheese
  spread with bacon
¼ cup beer
2 tablespoons chopped green onion
1 tablespoon chopped green pepper
1 tablespoon chopped pimento
1 teaspoon prepared horseradish
½ teaspoon prepared mustard

Yield: 2 Cups

Combine all ingredients in 1½-quart serving dish.

TO COOK BY INSTA-MATIC: Cover completely with plastic wrap. Cook on **COOK 8.**

TO COOK BY TIME: Cook at **HIGH** 3 to 4 minutes; stir once.

TO COMPLETE: Cheeses should be softened. Stir until well blended. Serve warm with assorted vegetable dippers.

53

APRICOT BRANDY

8 ounce package dried apricots, chopped
1 cup sugar
2 cups vodka

Yield: 2 Cups

Thoroughly combine all ingredients in medium glass bowl. Heat at **MEDIUM** 10 minutes, or until sugar is dissolved; stir twice. Heat at **WARM** 30 minutes; stir twice. Cover and let stand 3 to 4 days. Strain before serving.

PLUM BRANDY

1½ pounds fresh plums, halved (pits removed)
2 cups sugar
2 cups gin

Yield: 2 Cups

Thoroughly combine all ingredients in medium glass bowl. Heat at **MEDIUM** 10 minutes or until sugar is dissolved, stir once.
Heat at **WARM** 30 minutes; stir twice. Cover and let stand 3 to 4 days. Strain before serving.

COFFEE LIQUEUR

1½ cups hot water
2 cups sugar
⅓ cup freeze-dried coffee
2 cups vodka
1 vanilla bean

Yield: 2 Cups

Heat water in large glass bowl at **HIGH** 3 to 4 minutes, or until boiling. Stir in sugar and coffee until dissolved; add remaining ingredients. Heat at **MEDIUM** 5 minutes and at **WARM** 30 minutes; stir twice. Cover and let stand 3 to 4 days. Strain before serving.

PEACH LIQUEUR

1½ pounds fresh peaches, peeled and sliced
1½ cups sugar
4 strips lemon peel
3 whole cloves
2 cinnamon sticks
2 cups bourbon

Yield: 2 Cups

Thoroughly combine all ingredients in medium glass bowl. Heat at **MEDIUM** 10 minutes or until sugar is dissolved; stir once. Heat at **WARM** 30 minutes; stir twice. Cover and let stand 3 to 4 days. Strain before serving.

SAUCES and TOPPINGS

To add a special flair to your meals, try the recipes in this chapter. With the speedy assistance of your microwave oven, savory sauces and delicious dessert toppings to cook. Make a Creole Sauce to spice up left overs, or Hot Fudge Sauce for a late-night snack.

BASIC WHITE SAUCE I-M

2 tablespoons butter or margarine, melted
2 tablespoons flour
¼ teaspoon salt, optional
1 cup milk

Yield: 1 Cup

In 1½-quart bowl, combine melted butter, flour and salt. Gradually add milk; stir until smooth.

TO COOK BY INSTA-MATIC: Cover bowl completely with plastic wrap; cook on **COOK 8.** Stir when cooking is complete.

TO COOK BY TIME: Cook at **MEDIUM** 5 to 6 minutes, or until sauce is thickened. Stir occasionally with wire whisk.

Variations:
For CHEESE Sauce, stir in ½ to ¾ cup shredded cheese. Cook at MEDIUM 1 minute, if necessary, to completely melt cheese.
For CURRY Sauce, stir in 1 to 2 teaspoons curry powder.
For HORSERADISH Sauce, add 1 tablespoon prepared horseradish.
For MUSTARD Sauce, add 2 tablespoons prepared mustard and dash Worcestershire sauce.

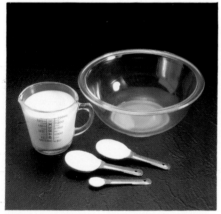

Melt butter at MEDIUM-LOW 30 seconds in 1½ quart bowl. Stir in flour and salt. Gradually add milk; stir until smooth.

To Cook by Time: Cook at MEDIUM 5 to 6 minutes, or until sauce is thickened.
To Cook by Insta-Matic: Cover completely with plastic wrap. Cook on COOK 8.

To Cook by Insta-Matic: Stir after cooking is completed.
To Cook by time: Stir occasionally with wire whisk.

BARBECUE SAUCE I-M

1 cup chili sauce
¾ cup water
¼ cup lemon juice
1 envelope (1⅜ oz.) onion soup mix
½ cup packed brown sugar
1 teaspoon dry mustard
⅛ teaspoon garlic powder

Yield: 2 Cups

Combine all ingredients in medium glass bowl.

TO COOK BY INSTA-MATIC: Cover completely with plastic wrap; cook on **COOK 3.** After time appears in display window, stir occasionally. After cooking, release plastic wrap.

TO COOK BY TIME: Cook at **HIGH** 5 minutes and at **MEDIUM-LOW** 8 to 10 minutes; stir occasionally.

TO COMPLETE: Sauce should be slightly thickened. Use as basting sauce on chicken, ribs, hamburgers, etc.

BORDELAISE SAUCE

2 tablespoons finely chopped onion
1 tablespoon butter or margarine
½ cup red wine
1 bay leaf
2 teaspoons cornstarch
½ cup beef broth
1 teaspoon butter
1 teaspoon parsley flakes

Yield: 1 Cup

Combine onion and butter in 2-cup glass measure. Cook at **HIGH** 1 to 1½ minutes; add wine and bay leaf. Cook at **HIGH** 3½ to 4 minutes, or until mixture is reduced to ⅓ cup. Strain and reserve wine. Blend cornstarch with broth until smooth. Stir into wine mixture. Cook at **HIGH** 2 to 2½ minutes, or until sauce is thickened; stir once. Stir in butter and parsley.

Variation: With broth, add 1 can (2 oz.) sliced mushrooms, drained.

JIFFY SPAGHETTI SAUCE

1 large onion, finely chopped
2 tablespoons oil
1 clove garlic, finely chopped
1 teaspoon oregano
⅛ teaspoon basil
2 cans (8 oz. ea.) tomato sauce
2 teaspoons sugar, optional

Yield: 2½ Cups

In medium glass bowl, combine onion, oil, garlic, oregano and basil. Cook, covered, at **HIGH** 2 to 2½ minutes, or until onion is tender; stir once. Stir in remaining ingredients and cook at **HIGH** 2 to 2½ minutes and at **MEDIUM-LOW** 4 to 5 minutes; stir once.

HOMEMADE GRAVY

1 to 2 tablespoons butter or margarine
2 tablespoons flour
Salt and pepper to taste
Few drops browning sauce, optional
1 cup roast drippings*

Yield: 1 Cup

Heat butter in small glass bowl at **HIGH** ½ to ¾ minute, or until melted. Stir in flour, salt, pepper and browning sauce. Gradually add drippings; stir until smooth. Cook at **HIGH** 2½ to 3½ minutes, or until gravy is thickened, stir twice.

*If necessary, add broth, milk or water to roast drippings to equal 1 cup. If using milk, cook at **MEDIUM** 3 to 4 minutes.*

CREOLE SAUCE

¼ cup finely chopped green pepper
1 small onion, finely chopped
¼ cup thinly sliced celery
2 tablespoons butter or margarine
1 teaspoon finely chopped garlic
¼ to ½ teaspoon chili powder
1 can (15 oz.) tomato sauce

Yield: 2½ Cups

In medium glass bowl, combine green pepper, onion, celery, butter, garlic and chili powder. Cook, covered with plastic wrap, at **HIGH** 2 to 3 minutes. Stir in tomato sauce; cook, covered, at **HIGH** 2 minutes, and at **MEDIUM-LOW** 4 to 5 minutes; stir once.

SWEET AND SOUR SAUCE

Water
**1 can (8¼ oz.) crushed pineapple in heavy
   syrup, drained; reserve syrup**
¼ cup packed brown sugar
1 tablespoon soy sauce, optional
1 tablespoon cornstarch
⅓ to ½ cup cider vinegar

Yield: 1½ Cups

In 2-cup glass measure, add enough water
to reserved syrup to equal ¾ cup; stir in
pineapple, brown sugar and soy sauce.
Cook at **HIGH** 2 to 2½ minutes; stir once.
Blend cornstarch with vinegar until
smooth. Stir into pineapple. Cook at **HIGH**
2 to 2½ minutes, or until sauce is slightly
thickened; stir once.

Variation: Add ½ cup finely chopped green
pepper with pineapple.

PREPARING CONVENIENCE SAUCES

- Use a glass container twice the volume of the sauce.
- Prepare sauce ingredients according to package directions.
- A wire whisk is helpful in eliminating lumps when stirring dry ingredients into liquids.
- If needed, melt butter **MEDIUM-LOW**.
- Cook sauces according to directions in chart.
- To blend flavors, when necessary, cook at **MEDIUM-LOW**.
- Stir occasionally during cooking.

RAISIN SAUCE FOR HAM ‖-M

½ cup orange juice
½ cup water
1 tablespoon cornstarch
1 tablespoon rum, optional
½ cup raisins
⅓ cup currant jelly*
Dash allspice

Yield: 1½ Cups

In 1½-quart glass bowl, stir together
orange juice, water and cornstarch until
blended. Stir in rum, raisins, currant jelly
and allspice.

TO COOK BY INSTA-MATIC: Cover
completely with plastic wrap; cook on
COOK 8. Stir before serving.

TO COOK BY TIME: Cook at **HIGH** 6 to 7
minutes, or until sauce is thickened. Stir
occasionally.

*****Substitution:** Use pineapple or apricot
preserves for currant jelly.*

ITEM	POWER	APPROX. COOKING TIME (in minutes)
Packaged Sauce and Gravy Mixes (¾ to 1½ oz.) prepared with water prepared with milk	HIGH MEDIUM	2½ to 3½ 3½ to 5
Sauces from condensed cream-style soups	MEDIUM	5 to 6
Spaghetti Sauce Mix (2 cup yield) prepared with tomato sauce prepared with tomato paste	HIGH→ M. LOW HIGH→ M.LOW	2½ to 3 8 to 10 2½ to 3 10 to 12

BANANA SPLIT TOPPING

1 can (8¼ oz.) chunk pineapple, drained; reserve syrup
1 can (17 oz.) dark sweet pitted cherries, drained; reserve syrup
1½ tablespoons cornstarch
2 bananas, cut into 1-inch pieces
Favorite flavors ice cream

Yield: 3 Cups

Reserve ¼ cup syrup. In medium glass bowl, combine remaining syrups, pineapple and cherries. Cook at **HIGH** 3 to 4 minutes; stir once. Blend cornstarch with reserved syrup until smooth. Stir into hot mixture. Cook at **HIGH** 2 to 2½ minutes, or until sauce is thickened; stir once. Cool slightly; slice bananas over ice cream and add topping.

ORANGE LIQUEUR SAUCE

½ cup water
¼ cup orange juice
3 to 4 tablespoons sugar
1 tablespoon cornstarch
1 to 2 tablespoons orange flavored liqueur

Yield: 1 Cup

In small glass bowl, combine water, orange juice, sugar and cornstarch. Cook at **HIGH** 1½ to 2 minutes, or until sauce is thickened; stir once. Stir in liqueur; cool. Serve, as desired, over rice pudding, chocolate mousse or plain cake.

BRANDIED CHERRY SAUCE

1 can (17 oz.) dark sweet pitted cherries, drained; reserve syrup
Water
½ cup sugar
1½ tablespoons cornstarch
¼ cup brandy

Yield: 6 Servings

Reserve ¼ cup syrup. To remaining syrup, add enough water to equal 1¼ cups. In medium glass bowl, combine syrup-water mixture, cherries and sugar. Cook at **HIGH** 3 to 4 minutes; stir once. Stir in cornstarch. Blend cornstarch with reserved syrup until smooth. Stir into hot mixture. Cook at **HIGH** 2 to 2½ minutes, or until sauce is thickened; stir once. Transfer to serving dish. Heat brandy in 1-cup glass measure at **HIGH** ½ to ¾ minute. Pour over cherries and carefully flame. Serve, as desired, over vanilla ice cream, angel food cake or chocolate soufflé.

CARAMEL SAUCE

1 package (14 oz.) caramels
2 tablespoons rum, optional
1 tablespoon water
¼ teaspoon cinnamon

Yield: 1¼ Cups

Combine all ingredients in small glass bowl. Cook at **HIGH** 3 to 4 minutes; stir until smooth.

LEMON SAUCE I-M

⅓ cup sugar
1½ tablespoons cornstarch
⅔ cup water
3 tablespoons lemon juice
Grated peel of 1 lemon
1 tablespoon butter or margarine

Yield: 1 Cup

Combine sugar and cornstarch in 2-cup glass measure. Stir in water, lemon juice and lemon peel; stir until sugar is dissolved.

TO COOK BY INSTA-MATIC: Cover completely with plastic wrap; cook on COOK 8.

TO COOK BY TIME: Cook at HIGH 2½ minutes.

TO COMPLETE: Stir in butter; cool slightly before serving.

VANILLA SAUCE

1 cup milk, divided
⅓ cup sugar
1½ tablespoons cornstarch
1 tablespoon butter or margarine
1 teaspoon vanilla

Yield: 1½ Cups

Combine ¾ cup milk and sugar in medium glass bowl. Cook at MEDIUM 3½ to 4 minutes, or until sugar is dissolved; stir once. Blend cornstarch with remaining milk until smooth. Stir into hot mixture. Cook at MEDIUM 2 to 2½ minutes, or until sauce is thickened; stir once. Stir in butter and vanilla; chill. Serve, as desired, in place of whipped cream. Delicious on fresh berries.

CUSTARD SAUCE

1½ cups milk
3 tablespoons sugar
2 tablespoons flour
2 egg yolks
1 teaspoon vanilla

Yield: 2 Cups

In medium glass bowl, combine milk, sugar and flour. Cook at MEDIUM 4 to 4½ minutes, or until sauce is slightly thickened; stir twice. With wire whip, quickly stir in egg yolks. Cook at MEDIUM-LOW 1 to 1½ minutes, or until sauce is thickened; stir twice. Stir in vanilla. Chill slightly before serving.

HOT FUDGE SAUCE

1 cup (6 oz.) semi-sweet chocolate pieces
½ cup light corn syrup
¼ cup half'n half or milk
1 tablespoon butter or margarine
1 teaspoon vanilla

Yield: 1½ Cups

Combine chocolate and syrup in small glass bowl. Cook at MEDIUM-LOW 4 to 4½ minutes; stir once. Gradually add half'n half, stir until smooth. Stir in butter and vanilla.

*Variation:
For CHOCOLATE MINT SAUCE, Use ½ to ¾ teaspoon mint extract for vanilla.

RUM SAUCE I-M

½ cup sugar
¼ cup butter or margarine
¼ cup evaporated milk
1 tablespoon rum extract
½ teaspoon vanilla

Yield: ½ Cup

Combine all ingredients in 2-cup glass measure.

TO COOK BY INSTA-MATIC: Cover completely with plastic wrap. Cook on COOK 8.

TO COOK BY TIME: Cook at HIGH 4 to 5 minutes.

TO COMPLETE: Stir. Let stand, covered, 5 minutes.

MELBA SAUCE I-M

1 package (10 oz.) frozen raspberries in heavy syrup, defrosted (see page 35)
1 can (8¼ oz.) sliced peaches, drained; reserve syrup
¼ cup water
1½ tablespoons cornstarch

Yield: 2 Cups

In small glass bowl, combine raspberries, reserved syrup, water and cornstarch.

TO COOK BY INSTA-MATIC: Cover completely with plastic wrap; cook on COOK 8.

TO COOK BY TIME: Cook at HIGH 4 to 4½ minutes, or until sauce is thickened; stir once.

TO COMPLETE: Stir well; chill. Just before serving, add peaches. Serve, as desired, over pound cake, ice cream or shortcake.

STRAWBERRY JAM

4 packages (10 oz. ea.) frozen strawberries in heavy syrup, defrosted (see page 35)
5 cups sugar
2 tablespoons lemon juice
½–6 ounce bottle liquid pectin

Yield: 6½ Cups

In 4-quart glass bowl, thoroughly combine strawberries, sugar and lemon juice. Cook at **HIGH** 20 to 22 minutes, or until mixture comes to a full boil; stir occasionally during first 7 minutes. Cook at **HIGH** an additional 1 minute. Stir in pectin and skim off any foam; stir and skim foam for about 7 minutes. Ladle into sterilized jars; seal with paraffin.

Note: Do not melt paraffin in your microwave oven.

Place defrosted strawberries 5 cups of sugar and lemon juice in 4-quart glass bowl.

Cook mixture at HIGH for 7 minutes. Stir 3 times during cooking.
Continue to cook at HIGH until mixture comes to a full boil about 13 to 15 minutes then cook an additional 1 minute.

Stir in pectin and skim off any foam. Continue to stir and skim foam for about 7 minutes.

Sterilize washed and rinsed jars by placing in pan with folded cloth or rack in bottom. Cover jars with water and boil 15 minutes on a CONVENTIONAL SURFACE UNIT. Jars should remain in this hot water until ready for use.

Ladle strawberry jam into hot sterilized jars. Seal with ⅛ to ¼-inch layer of paraffin. Store jellies and jams in a cook, dry place.

PEACH JAM

4 cups sliced, peeled fresh peaches
 (about 3 lb.)
7¼ cups sugar
¼ cup lemon juice
½–6 ounce bottle liquid pectin

Yield: 9 Cups

In 4-quart glass bowl, thoroughly combine peaches, sugar and lemon juice. Cook at **HIGH** 15 to 17 minutes, or until mixture comes to a full boil; stir occasionally during the first 5 minutes. Cook at **HIGH** an additional 1 minute. Stir in pectin and skim off any foam; stir and skim foam for about 7 minutes. Ladle into sterilized jars; seal with paraffin.

Note: *Do not melt paraffin in your microwave oven.*

GRAPE JELLY

2 cups grape juice
3½ cups sugar
½–6 ounce bottle liquid pectin

Yield: 3 Cups

Thoroughly combine juice and sugar in 4-quart glass bowl. Cook at **HIGH** 10 to 12 minutes, or until mixture is boiling; stir twice during first 4 minutes of heating. Stir in pectin. Cook at **HIGH** 4 to 6 minutes, or until mixture comes to a full boil. Cook at **HIGH** an additional 1 minute; skim off any foam. Ladle into sterilized jars; seal with paraffin.

APRICOT PINEAPPLE JAM

¼ pound dried apricots, finely chopped
1 can (20 oz.) crushed pineapple, drained (reserve syrup)
Water
6½ cups sugar
½ cup lemon juice
½–6 ounce bottle liquid pectin

Yield: 6½ Cups

Combine apricots and reserved syrup in 4-cup glass measure. Cook at **HIGH** 1 to 2 minutes, and at **MEDIUM** 3 to 4 minutes, or until apricots are soft.
Add pineapple and enough water to equal 3½ cups. In large bowl, thoroughly combine fruit mixture, sugar and lemon juice. Cook at **HIGH** 19 to 21 minutes, or until mixture comes to a full boil; stir occasionally during first 7 minutes. Cook at **HIGH** an additional 1 minute. Stir in pectin and skim off any foam; stir and skim foam for about 7 minutes. Ladle into sterilized jars; seal with paraffin.

Note: *Do not melt paraffin in your microwave oven.*

SOUPS and STEWS

Satisfy hearty appetites with savory soups and stews prepared in your microwave oven. The lower power levels, MEDIUM-LOW and LOW allow flavors to blend and less tender cuts of meat to become tender. Follow our recipes for homemade soups and stew or adapt your favorites by using similar cooking power, times and techniques.

BEEF STEW

2 pounds boneless beef, cut into 1-inch cubes
2 cups water, divided
1 envelope (1¾ oz.) onion soup mix
4 medium carrots, thinly sliced
2 potatoes (about 8 oz. ea.) peeled and cut into ½-inch cubes
1 bay leaf
1 can (8 oz.) green peas, drained
¼ cup flour

Yield: 8 Servings

In 4-quart casserole, combine beef, 1½ cups water, soup mix, carrots, potatoes and bay leaf. Cover with lid. Cook at **HIGH** 8 minutes and at **MEDIUM-LOW** 55 to 60 minutes, or until beef is tender; stir occasionally.
Add peas. Blend flour with remaining ½ cup water. Cook at **HIGH** 5 to 7 minutes, or until stew is thickened; stir occasionally. Remove bay leaf before serving.

In 4-quart casserole, combine beef, 1½ cups water, soup mix, carrots, potatoes and bay leaf.

Cover with lid. Cook on HIGH for 8 minutes and at MEDIUM-LOW 55 to 60 minutes, or until beef is tender, stir occasionally.

Add peas. Blend flour with remaining ½ cup water. Stir into stew. Cook at HIGH 5 to 7 minutes, or until stew is thickened; stir occasionally.

CHILI STEW I-M

1 pound lean ground beef
2 medium onions, chopped
¼ teaspoon dried garlic pieces
1 can (16 oz.) pinto or red kidney beans
1 can (15 oz.) stewed tomatoes, chopped
1 can (15 oz.) tomato sauce
1 teaspoon salt
2 to 3 tablespoons chili powder

Yield: 4 Servings

TO COOK BY INSTA-MATIC: Crumble ground beef in 3-quart casserole. Stir in remaining ingredients. Cover; cook on **COOK 2**. After time appears in display window, stir occasionally.

TO COOK BY TIME: Crumble ground beef in 3-quart casserole. Stir in onion and garlic. Cook at **HIGH** 6 to 7 minutes. Stir once; drain. Stir in remaining ingredients. Cover with lid. Cook at **HIGH** 7 minutes and at **MEDIUM-LOW** 35 to 40 minutes; stir occasionally.

TO COMPLETE: Stir. Let stand, covered, 7 minutes before serving.

BAVARIAN STEW

1½ pounds round steak, cut into strips
2 cups water, divided
2 medium onions, sliced
¼ cup cider vinegar
1 tablespoon sugar
1 bay leaf
1 teaspoon salt
½ teaspoon caraway seeds
1 small head (about 1 lb.) red cabbage, shredded*
¼ cup flour

Yield: 6 Servings

In 4-quart casserole, combine meat, 1½ cups water, onions, vinegar, sugar, bay leaf, salt and caraway. Cover with lid. Cook at **HIGH** 7 minutes and at **LOW** 30 to 35 minutes; stir occasionally.
Add red cabbage. Cook, covered, at **LOW** 20 to 25 minutes, or until beef and cabbage are tender; stir occasionally.
Blend flour with remaining ½ cup water until smooth. Stir into hot mixture. Cook at **HIGH** 4 to 5 minutes, or until stew is thickened; stir once.

Substitution: *Use 1 jar (16 oz.) red cabbage, drained, for fresh red cabbage.*

ZESTY BEEF STEW

2 tablespoons flour
1 teaspoon salt
¼ teaspoon pepper
¼ teaspoon garlic powder
1½ pounds round steak, cut into 1-inch
    cubes
1 large onion, sliced
½ cup chopped green pepper
½ cup catsup
¼ cup packed brown sugar

Yield: 4–6 Servings

In small dish combine flour, salt, pepper
and garlic powder. Coat meat with flour
mixture. In 2-quart casserole, combine
meat, onion, green pepper, catsup and
sugar. Cover with lid.
Cook at **MEDIUM** 10 minutes and at
MEDIUM-LOW 20 to 22 minutes, or until
meat is tender. Stir occasionally. Let stand,
covered, 5 minutes. Serve, if desired, over
noodles.

IRISH STEW I-M

2 pounds boneless lamb, cut into 1-inch
    cubes
2 medium carrots, sliced into ¼-inch
    pieces
2 potatoes (about 6 oz. ea.), peeled and
    cubed
2½ cups hot water, divided
1 envelope (1 oz.) onion-mushroom soup
    mix
1 bay leaf
¼ cup flour

Yield: 8 Servings

In 4-quart casserole, arrange lamb, carrots
and potatoes forming three separate layers.
In bowl, combine 2 cups hot water, soup
mix and bay leaf. Stir together until well
blended. Pour mixture over potatoes. Cover
with lid.

TO COOK BY INSTA-MATIC: Cook on
COOK 2. After time appears in display
window, stir twice.

TO COOK BY TIME: Cook at **HIGH** 7
minutes and at **LOW** 70 to 75 minutes. Stir
twice.

TO COMPLETE: Blend flour with remaining
½ cup water until smooth. Stir into dish.*
Cook at **HIGH** 4 to 5 minutes, or until stew
is thickened.

*If desired, add ¼ teaspoon browning
    sauce.

76

APPLE CIDER STEW I-M

½ small turnip, diced (about 3 cups)
½ pound fresh green beans, cut into
  1½-inch pieces*
½ cup water, divided
1 cup sliced onion
2 pounds boneless beef, cut into 1-inch
  cubes
2 cups apple cider
2 tablespoons catsup
2 teaspoons salt
1 bay leaf
¼ teaspoon pepper
⅛ teaspoon thyme
¼ cup flour

Yield: 8 Servings

TO COOK BY INSTA-MATIC: In 4-quart
casserole, combine, turnips, beans, ¼ cup
water, onion, beef, apple cider, catsup,
salt, bay leaf, pepper and thyme; mix well.
Cover with lid. Cook on **COOK 2**. After time
appears in display window, stir
occasionally.

TO COOK BY TIME: In medium glass bowl,
combine turnips, beans and ¼ cup water.
Cook at **HIGH** 8 to 9 minutes; stir once.
Drain; reserve vegetables. In 4-quart
casserole, combine onion, beef, cider,
catsup, salt, bay leaf, pepper and thyme.
Cover with lid. Cook at **HIGH** 5 to 6
minutes and at **LOW** 60 minutes. Stir
occasionally.
Add reserved vegetables and cook,
covered, at **LOW** 15 minutes or until
tender.

TO COMPLETE: Blend flour with remaining
¼ cup water until smooth. Stir into stew.
Cook at **HIGH** 3 to 4 minutes, or until stew
is slightly thickened. Stir once.

*Substitution: Use 1 can (16 oz.) sliced
  potatoes, drained, and 1 can (16 oz.)
  sliced green beans, drained. Do not
  precook, just add to stew.*

TERRIFIC BEER STEW I-M

1½ pounds boneless beef, cut into 1-inch
  cubes
4 carrots, cut into ½-inch slices
1 can (10½ oz.) beef broth
1 cup beer
1 tablespoon packed brown sugar
1½ teaspoon salt
1 teaspoon thyme
½ teaspoon pepper
3 medium onions, cut in eighths
1 package (10 oz.) frozen green peas
¼ cup water
3 tablespoons flour
1 regular size (10×16-inch) oven cooking
  bag

Yield: 6 Servings

TO COOK BY INSTA-MATIC: In 4-quart
casserole (do NOT use cooking bag),
combine beef, carrots, beef broth, beer,
sugar, salt, thyme, pepper and onions.
Cover with lid. Cook on **COOK 2**. After time
appears in the display window, add peas.
Stir occasionally.

TO COOK BY TIME: Prepare cooking bag
according to package directions. In cooking
bag, combine beef, carrots, beef broth,
beer, sugar, salt, thyme, pepper and
onions. Turn bag several times to mix. Pull
bag up around beef and close (3-inch from
top) with nylon tie or cotton string. Make
six half-inch slits in top of bag. Place in 2-
quart casserole. Cook at **HIGH** 7 minutes
and at **LOW** 30 minutes. Open bag, add
peas, and reclose bag. Cook at **LOW** 20 to
30 minutes.

TO COMPLETE: Blend flour with water*
until smooth. Stir into stew. Cook at **HIGH**
2 to 2½ minutes, or until slightly
thickened.

*If desired, add ½ teaspoon browning
  sauce.*

FISHERMAN'S POT

1 can (28 oz.) whole tomatoes, chopped
1 cup chicken broth
½ cup thinly sliced celery
1 large onion, sliced
1 tablespoon sugar, optional
1 teaspoon parsley flakes
1 teaspoon salt
Dash thyme
1 pound fish fillets, cut into chunks*
¼ cup white wine, optional

Yield: 4 Servings

In 3-quart casserole, combine tomatoes, broth, celery, onion, sugar, garlic, parsley, salt and thyme. Cover with lid. Cook at **HIGH** 5 minutes and at **MEDIUM** 9 to 10 minutes; stir once. Add fish and wine. Cook, covered, at **MEDIUM** 10 minutes, or until fish is tender, stir once. Let stand, covered, 5 minutes before serving.

***Variation:** Use a combination of your favorite fish.*

BRUNSWICK STEW

2½ to 3 pound chicken, cut into serving
  pieces
1 can (16 oz.) whole tomatoes, chopped
1¼ cups water, divided
1 medium onion, thinly sliced
2 teaspoons salt
2 bay leaves, crushed
¼ teaspoon pepper
1 package (10 oz.) frozen succotash,
  partially defrosted (see page 35)
1 package (10 oz.) frozen sliced okra,
  partially defrosted (see page 35)
¼ cup flour

Yield: 4 Servings

In 3-quart casserole, combine chicken, tomatoes, 1 cup water, onion, salt, bay leaves and pepper. Cover with lid. Cook at **HIGH** 7 minutes and at **MEDIUM** 14 to 16 minutes. Stir once.
Stir in succotash and okra; recover. Cook at **HIGH** 10 to 12 minutes; stir once. Blend flour with remaining ¼ cup water until smooth. Stir into liquid. Cook at **HIGH** 5 to 6 minutes, or until thickened.

SPICY SAUSAGE STEW

1 pound Italian sausage links, cut into
  1½-inch pieces
1 pound boneless pork, cut into 1-inch
  cubes
1 can (28 oz.) whole tomatoes, chopped
1 can (8 oz.) tomato sauce
1 green pepper, cut into chunks
1 teaspoon basil
1 teaspoon oregano
½ teaspoon garlic powder

Yield: 6 Servings

Cook sausage in 3-quart casserole at **HIGH** 5 to 6 minutes; stir once. Drain. Stir in remaining ingredients. Cover with lid. Cook at **HIGH** 5 minutes and at **LOW** 55 to 60 minutes, or until pork is tender. Stir occasionally. Skim off fat from liquid. Serve, if desired, with rice or pasta.

Most roasts can be cooked rare, medium or even
well-done in less than one hour. Less tender cuts
of meat such as pot roast can be simmered fork-
tender in a sauce or gravy by using LOW power.
In this chapter, there are a variety of recipes to
please everyone, everyday favorites, entertaining
specials and calorie savers. Use these times
and procedures as well as the information
from the charts as a guideline when
microwaving a favorite recipe for
the first time.

GENERAL DIRECTIONS FOR ROASTING TENDER CUTS OF MEAT

For best results, select roasts that are uniform in shape.

Season as desired, but salt after cooking. Browning sauce mixed with equal parts of butter will enhance the color.

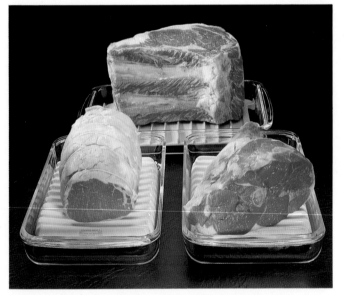

Place meat on microwave roasting rack set in a 12×8 inch dish. Beef Rib roast should be placed cut side down. Other roasts should be placed fat-side down. Halfway through cooking turn roasts over.

Meats can be shielded at the beginning of cooking or halfway through cooking. If you wish to shield at the beginning of cooking, remove foil halfway through the cooking time. Beef and pork rib roasts should be shielded by the bones. Foil should extend about 2-inches down from bones. The shank bone on a lamb roast should be cupped with foil. Thin ends of boneless roasts should also be shielded.

Half hams should be shielded by wrapping a 3-inch wide strip of foil around the large end of the ham. Secure to the body of the ham with wooden toothpicks. Fold 1½ inches over cut surface. For shank ham halves, shield shank bone by cupping it with foil.

One-third of the way through cooking, remove ham from oven and cut off skin. Turn fat-side up and reshield edges. If desired, glaze last 10 to 20 minutes of cooking.

Canned hams should be shielded on the top cut-edge with a 1½-inch strip of foil. Wrap strip of foil around ham and secure to body of ham with wooden toothpicks. Fold 1-inch over cut surface. If desired, glaze last 10 to 20 minutes of cooking.

Loosely cover baking dish with wax paper to prevent spatter. If a large amount of juice accumulates in the bottom of the dish, drain occasionally. If desired, reserve for making gravy.

To Cook by Time:
Multiply the weight of the roast by the minimum number of minutes per pound. Recommended in chart on page 83.

To Cook by Temperature Probe:
Insert probe into meat as horizontally as possible. Probe tip should be in center of meat, but not touching bone or fatty area. Set Insta-Matic Temperature or Programmable Temperature as indicated in recipe, or chart on page 83.

After cooking, check internal temperature of the roast in several places, using a microwave or conventional meat thermometer. The thermometer should not touch bone or fat. If it does, the reading could be inaccurate. Generally, the lower temperatures in a roast are found in the center of the roast and in the muscle close to a large bone, such as a pork loin center rib roast. If the temperatures are lower than desired, return the roast to the oven and cook a few more minutes at the recommended power level. DO NOT USE A CONVENTIONAL MEAT THERMOMETER IN THE MICROWAVE OVEN.
Let stand, tented with foil, 10 to 15 minutes. During stand time internal temperature rises 5°F to 15°F.

82

MEAT ROASTING CHART FOR TIME COOKING

MEAT	POWER	APPROX. COOKING TIME (minutes per pound)	APPROX. TEMPERATURE AFTER STANDING
Beef Roasts (up to 5 lb.) Rare Medium Well	MEDIUM-LOW MEDIUM-LOW MEDIUM-LOW	8½ to 9½ 11 to 12½ 13 to 14½	125° to 135°F 135° to 145°F 170° to 175°F
Beef Pot Roast (up to 4 lb.) *Chuck, Rump, Flank	LOW	20 to 25	———————
Pork Roast (up to 5 lb.) Ham (fully cooked) Canned (3 to 5 lb.) Shank (8 lb.) Chops ½" thick	MEDIUM-LOW MEDIUM-LOW MEDIUM-LOW MEDIUM	12 to 13½ 9 to 10 9 to 10 8 to 11	170° to 175°F 120° to 130°F 120° to 130°F ———————
Lamb Roast (up to 5 lb.) Medium Well Chops ½" thick	MEDIUM-LOW MEDIUM-LOW MEDIUM	11 to 12½ 13 to 14½ 7 to 10	150° to 160°F 170° to 175°F ———————

These meats should be cooked in an oven cooking bag or covered casserole surrounded with liquid.

MEAT ROASTING CHART FOR TEMPERATURE PROBE

MEAT	INSTA-MATIC TEMP SETTING	PROGRAMMABLE TEMPERATURE		APPROXIMATE TEMPERATURE AFTER STANDING
		FIRST-STAGE POWER & TEMP	SECOND-STAGE POWER & TEMP	
Beef Roasts Rare Medium Well	TEMP 1 TEMP 2 TEMP 3	MEDIUM-LOW 100°F MEDIUM-LOW 100°F → MEDIUM-LOW 100°F →	——————— LOW 110°F LOW 160°F	125° to 135°F 135° to 145°F 170° to 175°F
Pork Roast (up to 5 lb.) Ham (fully cooked) Canned (3 to 5 lb.) Shank (8 lb.)	TEMP 6 —— ——	MEDIUM-LOW 100°F → MEDIUM-LOW 100°F → MEDIUM-LOW 100°F →	LOW 170°F LOW 120°F LOW 120°F	170° to 175°F 120° to 130°F 120° to 130°F
Lamb Roast (up to 5 lb.) Medium Well	TEMP 4 TEMP 5	MEDIUM-LOW 100°F → MEDIUM-LOW 100°F →	LOW 130°F LOW 170°F	150° to 160°F 170° to 175°F

DIRECTIONS FOR COOKING LESS TENDER CUTS BY TIME

Less tender cuts such as pot roasts should be cooked in liquid. Use ½ to 1 cup of soup, broth, etc. Use an oven cooking bag or covered casserole when cooking less tender cuts of meat. Select a covered casserole deep enough so that the meat does not touch the lid.

If an oven cooking bag is used, prepare the bag according to package directions. Do not use wire or metal twist-ties. Use the nylon tie provided, otherwise, use a piece of cotton string or a strip cut from the open end of the bag. Make six ½-inch slits in top of bag to allow steam to escape.

Multiply the weight of the roast by the minimum number of minutes per pound recommended in chart of page 83. Program oven. Turn meat over halfway through cooking. Meat should be fork tender when done.

DIRECTIONS FOR COOKING LESS TENDER CUTS BY INSTA-MATIC

Less tender cuts such as pot roasts should be cooked in liquid. Use 1 cup of liquid, such as soup or broth, per pound of meat. Cook in a 4-quart covered casserole. Do not use an oven cooking bag.

Cook on COOK 2. When time appears in display window turn meat over. Meat should be fork tender when done.

GENERAL DIRECTIONS FOR PREPARING CONVENIENCE MEATS

Brush hamburgers and fresh sausage links with browning sauce mixed with equal parts of melted butter to enhance appearance.

Pierce sausage links with fork and score frankfurters before cooking.

To Cook by Time:

Arrange food in a single layer in baking dish. Loosely cover with wax paper to prevent spatter. Up to four slices of bacon may be placed between layers of paper towels on paper plate. Cook according to time given in chart on page 87.

Let stand according to recommended time in charts.

To Cook by Insta-Matic

Arrange food in a single layer in baking dish. Cover completely with plastic wrap. Cook on Insta-Matic setting as indicated in chart on page 87.

After cooking release plastic wrap and let stand as indicated in chart before serving.

| ITEM | AMOUNT | TIME COOKING | | | INSTA-MATIC COOKING |
		POWER	APPROX. COOKING TIME (in minutes)	STAND TIME (in minutes)	
Bacon, slices*	2 3 4 8	HIGH	1 to 1½ 1½ to 2 2 to 3 4½ to 5½	1 1 1 1	———
Canadian bacon slices (2 oz. ea.)	2 4 8	HIGH	½ to 1 1 to 1½ 2 to 2½	3 3 3	COOK 8 COOK 8
Frankfurters, scored	2 4	HIGH	1½ to 2 2½ to 3½	3 3	COOK 8 COOK 8
Ham, slices (about 2 oz. ea.)	2 4	HIGH	1½ to 2½ 2½ to 3½	3 3	———
Hamburgers, frozen (4 oz. ea.)	1 2 4	M. HIGH	2 to 2½ 3½ to 4½ 5½ to 6½	2 3 3	FROZEN FOODS 3 FROZEN FOODS 3 FROZEN FOODS 3
Hamburgers (4 oz. ea.)	1 2 4	M. HIGH	1 to 2½ 2 to 2½ 3½ to 4	2 2 2	COOK 7 COOK 7 COOK 7
Sausage Links, frozen, (precooked, brown and serve)	2 4 8	HIGH	1 to 1½ 1½ to 2 3 to 4	2 2 2	———
Sausage Links, + fresh (2 oz. ea.)	2 4 8	HIGH	2 to 3 4 to 5 7 to 8	3 3 3	———
Sausage Patties fresh (1 to 2 oz. ea.)	2 4	HIGH	1 to 2½ 2 to 4	2 2	COOK 3

*Note: Cooking more than 4 pieces bacon on paper utensils at one time is not recommended.
†Special Hint: Pierce with fork and brush with browning sauce before cooking.

BEEF WITH BROCCOLI

1 tablespoon oil
1 pound boneless steak, cut into thin strips
1 clove garlic, finely chopped
⅛ teaspoon ginger
3 to 4 cups broccoli flowerets
1 tablespoon cornstarch
½ cup beef broth
1 tablespoon sherry
1 tablespoon soy sauce
Toasted sesame seeds (see page 235)

Yield: 4 Servings

Heat oil in 12×8-inch dish at **HIGH** 2 minutes. Stir in beef, garlic and ginger. Cook at **HIGH** 3½ to 4½ minutes; stir twice. Add broccoli. Cook, covered with plastic wrap, at **HIGH** 5 to 6 minutes, or until broccoli is crisp tender; stir once. Blend cornstarch with broth, sherry and soy sauce until smooth. Stir into beef mixture. Cook at **HIGH** 3 to 4 minutes, or until sauce is thickened; stir once. Top with sesame seeds.

Hint: *If desired, combine beef with garlic, ginger, broth, sherry and soy sauce; marinate 30 minutes. Drain and reserve marinade to thicken. Proceed as directed above.*

BEEF STROGANOFF

3 tablespoons butter or margarine
1 large onion, thinly sliced
1 pound boneless steak, cut into thin strips
¼ pound fresh mushrooms, sliced
Beef broth
½ teaspoon salt
¼ teaspoon pepper
2 tablespoons flour
½ to 1 cup sour cream or plain yogurt
⅛ teaspoon browning sauce, optional

Yield: 4 Servings

Heat butter in 12×8-inch dish at **HIGH** 1½ to 2 minutes. Add onion. Cook at **HIGH** 2 to 2½ minutes; stir once. Add beef and mushrooms. Cook at **MEDIUM-HIGH** 6½ to 7 minutes; stir twice. Drain and reserve liquid; add enough broth to reserved liquid to equal ¾ cup. Sprinkle beef with salt and pepper. Into dish, blend in flour, then broth mixture. Cook at **MEDIUM** 2½ to 3 minutes, or until sauce is thickened. Blend in sour cream and browning sauce and heat, if necessary, at **MEDIUM** 2 to 3 minutes.

Note: ***For TWO Servings,*** *following above procedure; halve all ingredients. Heat butter 1 minute, onion 1 to 1¼ minutes, beef 3 to 3½ minutes and sauce 1 to 1½ minutes.*

TERIYAKI BEEF KABOBS

2 tablespoons packed brown sugar
2 tablespoons soy sauce
1 tablespoon lemon juice
1 tablespoon oil
1 pound boneless steak, cut into
   1½-inch cubes
½ pint cherry tomatoes
1 medium green pepper, cut into chunks

Yield: 4 Servings

In bowl, combine sugar, soy sauce, lemon juice and oil; add steak. If desired, cover and marinate in refrigerator at least 3 hours, stirring occasionally. On four 9 or 10-inch wooden skewers, alternately thread steak, tomatoes and green pepper. Arrange skewers on 8-inch square baking dish. Cook at **MEDIUM** 7 to 9* minutes.

Cooking time given is for beef Medium-Rare. Adjust time accordingly for desired doneness.
Note: *If wooden skewers are unavailable, metal skewers may be used. Refer to page 9 for special instructions.*

BEST BEEF GOULASH I-M

2 pounds boneless beef, cut into 1-inch
   cubes
2¼ cups water, divided
1 envelope (1⅜ oz.) onion soup mix
1 can (3 oz.) whole mushrooms, drained
2 tablespoons paprika
¼ teaspoon caraway seeds
3 tablespoons cornstarch

Yield: 6–8 Servings

In 4-quart casserole, combine beef, 2 cups water, onion soup mix, mushrooms, paprika and caraway seeds. Cover with lid.

TO COOK BY INSTA-MATIC: Cook on **COOK 2**. After time appears in display window, stir twice.

TO COOK BY TIME: Cook at **HIGH** 6 minutes and at **LOW** 55 to 60 minutes; stir twice.

TO COMPLETE: Blend cornstarch with remaining ¼ cup water until smooth. Stir into dish. Cook, uncovered, at **LOW** 3 minutes, or until thickened.

MUSHROOM STUFFED STEAK I-M ROLLS

¼ pound fresh mushrooms, finely chopped
1 small onion, finely chopped
2 tablespoons butter or margarine
2 cups soft bread crumbs
1 tablespoon parsley flakes
1 to 1½ pounds thin cut top round steak,
   cut into 4 pieces
Salt and pepper to taste
1 can (10¼ oz.) beef gravy

Yield: 4 Servings

In medium glass bowl, combine mushrooms, onion and butter. Cook at **HIGH** 2 to 3 minutes. Stir in bread crumbs and parsley flakes.
Pound steak thin for rolling*. Season one side with salt and pepper. Place mushroom mixture on seasoned side of each steak and roll up jelly roll style. Tie with cotton string or secure with wooden toothpicks. In a 8-inch square dish, arrange rolls around edge of dish; top with gravy. Cover completely with plastic wrap.

TO COOK BY INSTA-MATIC: Cook on **COOK 3**. After time appears in the display window turn rolls over.

TO COOK BY TIME: Cook at **HIGH** 5 minutes and at **MEDIUM** 10 to 12 minutes. Turn rolls over, halfway through cooking.

TO COMPLETE: After cooking, release plastic wrap. Let stand, covered, 5 minutes before serving.

Hint: In some markets steaks may be purchased ready for rolling.

FILET AU JUS

4 beef tenderloin steaks, 1-inch thick
   (about ¼ lb. ea.)
½ teaspoon pepper
4 slices bacon
Browning sauce

Yield: 4 Servings

Rub steaks with pepper; wrap bacon around steaks and secure bacon with wooden toothpicks. In 12×8-inch dish, arrange steaks; brush with browning sauce. Cook at **MEDIUM** 6 to 7 minutes*, turning steaks over halfway through cooking. Let stand, covered, 2 to 4 minutes before serving.

Cooking time given is for beef-Rare. For Medium, cook 8 to 9 minutes and for Well, cook 10 to 11 minutes.

Note: For TWO Servings, *follow above procedure; halve all ingredients. Cook 3½ to 4½ minutes (for Rare), 4½ to 5½ (for Medium) or 5½ to 6½ (for Well).*

FLORENTINE FLANK STEAK **I-M**

1¼ to 1½ pound beef flank steak,
   pounded thin
¼ pound fresh mushrooms
2 tablespoons finely chopped onion
1 clove garlic, finely chopped
2 tablespoons butter or margarine
1 package (10 oz.) frozen chopped spinach,
   defrosted and well drained (see page 35)
1 can (10¾ oz.) condensed golden
   mushroom soup
⅓ cup water

Yield: 4 Servings

Score one side of steak in diamond pattern. Chop ½ cup mushrooms. In medium glass bowl, combine mushrooms, onion, garlic and butter; cook at **HIGH** 2 to 3 minutes or until onions are tender. Add spinach; stir. Spread spinach mixture on unscored side of steak, roll-up jelly roll fashion starting with narrow end. Secure with wooden toothpicks. Place seam side down in 12×8-inch dish. In 4-cup glass measure, combine soup and water. Stir until smooth. Add remaining mushrooms, sliced. Pour over steak.

TO COOK BY INSTA-MATIC: Cover dish completely with plastic wrap, taking care that the toothpicks don't pierce it. Cook on **COOK 2.** After time appears in display window, turn meat over, spoon sauce over top. After cooking, release plastic wrap.

TO COOK BY TIME: Cover meat with wax paper. Cook at **MEDIUM** for 7 minutes and **MEDIUM-LOW** for 30 minutes. Halfway through cooking, turn meat over and spoon sauce over top.

TO COMPLETE: Let stand, covered, 5 minutes before serving. Slice diagonally into thin strips. Serve sauce with steak.

SWISS STEAK SPECIAL

1½ pounds boneless round steak, cut into individual servings and pounded ¼-inch thin
1 can (16 oz.) whole tomatoes, chopped
1 can (8 oz.) tomato sauce
1 envelope (1⅜ oz.) onion or onion-mushroom soup mix
1 teaspoon basil
¼ teaspoon garlic powder
6 slices (6 oz.) mozzarella cheese

Yield: 6 Servings

In 12×8-inch dish, combine steak, tomatoes, sauce, soup mix, basil and garlic. Cover with plastic wrap. Cook at **HIGH** 5 minutes and at **LOW** 40 to 45 minutes. Top with cheese. Let stand, covered, 10 minutes before serving.

SHORT RIBS WITH BARBECUE SAUCE

4 pounds beef short ribs
1 medium onion, sliced
2 stalks celery, sliced
1¼ cups catsup
¼ cup packed brown sugar
¼ cup cider vinegar
¼ cup flour
1 tablespoon Worcestershire sauce
½ teaspoon salt
¼ teaspoon dry mustard

Yield: 4 Servings

In 12×8-inch dish, arrange ribs, meatiest portions toward edge of dish. Add onion and celery. Cook, covered with plastic wrap, at **MEDIUM** 10 to 15 minutes. Drain. Meanwhile, combine remaining ingredients. Pour over ribs. Cook, covered, at **HIGH** 5 minutes and at **LOW** 60 minutes, or until ribs are tender. Rearrange ribs once and baste with sauce occasionally. Let stand, covered, 5 minutes, before serving.

CORNED BEEF DINNER

6 medium new potatoes (about 5 oz. ea.)
2½ to 3 pound corned beef brisket
2 onions, quartered
1½ cups water
1 small head cabbage (about 1½ lb.), cut into 6 wedges
1 regular size (10″×16″) oven cooking bag

Yield: 6 Servings

Following the method for baking potatoes (page 167), cook potatoes 11 to 12 minutes. Cool, then peel.
Meanwhile, prepare cooking bag according to package directions. Place corned beef, onion and water in bag. Set bag in 12×8-inch dish. Pull bag up around beef. Close bag with nylon tie or cotton string. Make 6 (½-in.) slits in top of bag. Cook at **HIGH** 6 minutes and at **LOW** 90 minutes, or until beef is tender. Remove to serving platter. Let stand, covered, 15 minutes.
Meanwhile, in same dish, arrange cabbage (thick sides toward edge of dish) and potatoes. Add ½ cup cooking liquid. Cook, covered, with plastic wrap at **HIGH** 9 to 11 minutes, or until cabbage and potatoes are tender. Slice corned beef and serve with vegetables.

91

ITALIAN BEEF

3 to 4 pound beef rump roast, thinly sliced*
1 can (4 oz.) mushrooms
1 medium onion, chopped
¼ cup chopped green pepper
2 bay leaves
1 clove garlic, finely chopped
1 teaspoon salt
1 can (17 oz.) tomatoes
1 can (10½ oz.) condensed beef broth
½ cup dry red wine
1 jar (8 oz.) mild giardinera, undrained**

Yield: 8–10 Servings

Arrange sliced beef in 2½-quart casserole. Combine remaining ingredients and pour over meat.

TO COOK BY TEMPERATURE: Insert temperature probe into liquid. Cover with lid. Set on Insta-Matic **TEMP 8**. After the selected temperature is reached, oven will automatically hold at 190°F for 2½ hours. Stir occasionally.

TO COOK BY TIME: Cover with lid. Cook 1½ hours at **MEDIUM-LOW** and 2½ hours at **LOW**. Stir occasionally.

TO COMPLETE: Serve on Italian bread.

*For easier slicing, partially freeze beef.
**Assorted peppers, celery, olives, capers, pimento and spices packed in oil.

PEPPER STEAK

2 tablespoons oil
1 pound boneless beef sirloin steak, cut into thin strips
2 tablespoons soy sauce
Dash ginger
Salt to taste
2 medium green peppers, cut into chunks
2 medium onions, sliced
1 tablespoon cornstarch
½ cup beef broth

Yield: 4 Servings

Heat oil in 12×8-inch dish at **MEDIUM-HIGH** 2 minutes. Add steak, soy sauce and ginger. Cook at **MEDIUM-HIGH** 5 to 6 minutes; stir once. Season with salt and stir in peppers and onions. Cook, covered with plastic wrap, at **MEDIUM-HIGH** 3 to 3½ minutes, or until vegetables are crisp-tender.

Blend cornstarch with broth until smooth. Stir into dish. Cook at **MEDIUM-HIGH** 3 to 3½ minutes, or until sauce is thickened; stir once.

Note: *For TWO Servings, follow above procedure; halve all ingredients. Heat oil 1 minute, steak 2 to 2½ minutes, vegetables 1½ to 2 minutes and broth 1½ to 2 minutes.*

SWEET 'N SOUR FLANK STEAK

1 cup unsweetened pineapple juice
2 tablespoons cider vinegar
1 can (8 oz.) tomato sauce
2 teaspoons Worcestershire sauce
1 pound beef flank steak, pounded thin and and scored
1 large onion, sliced
1 green pepper, cut into slivers
1½ tablespoons cornstarch
2 tablespoons water

Yield: 4 Servings

Combine pineapple juice, cider vinegar, tomato sauce and Worcestershire; set aside. Place meat in 12×8-inch dish. Top with onions and green peppers. Pour sauce over meat. Cover with plastic wrap. Cook at **MEDIUM-LOW** 23 to 25 minutes, or until meat is tender. Halfway through cooking, turn meat over.
Place meat and vegetables on serving dish. Pour sauce into 4-cup glass measure. Blend cornstarch with water until smooth. Stir into sauce. Cook at **HIGH** 4 to 5 minutes; stir twice. Pour over meat and serve immediately.

RANCHERO POT ROAST I-M

1 teaspoon garlic salt
½ to 1 teaspoon pepper
¼ to 1 teaspoon paprika
3 to 3¼ pound bottom round roast
1 can (10¼ oz.) beef broth
½ cup chili sauce
2 tablespoons dried onion flakes

Yield: 8 Servings

Combine garlic salt, pepper and paprika; rub over roast. Place meat in 3-quart casserole. Combine remaining ingredients; pour over meat. Cover with lid.

TO COOK BY INSTA-MATIC: Cook on **COOK 2**. After time appears in display window, turn meat over; cover.

TO COOK BY TIME: Cook at **HIGH** 5 minutes and at **LOW** 90 minutes. Halfway through cooking time turn meat over; cover.

TO COMPLETE: Beef should be tender. Let stand, covered, 10 minutes before serving.

Hint: If thicker gravy is desired, remove roast to serving platter. Let stand, covered. Pour gravy into microwave safe bowl. Blend 3 to 4 tablespoons flour with ½ cup water until smooth. Stir into gravy. Heat at HIGH 3 to 4 minutes; stir once.

CHILI BEEF LIVER

6 slices bacon
1 pound beef liver, thinly sliced
2 tablespoons flour
1 can (10½ oz.) condensed onion soup
1 can (4 oz.) sliced mushrooms, drained
¼ cup chili sauce or catsup

Yield: 4 Servings

In 12×8-inch dish, arrange bacon. Cook, covered with paper towel, at **HIGH** 4½ to 5½ minutes. Remove bacon; crumble and reserve. In dish, arrange liver lightly coated with flour; cook at **HIGH** 1 to 2 minutes. Turn liver over; add soup, mushrooms and chili sauce. Cook, covered, with plastic wrap, at **HIGH** 5 minutes and at **MEDIUM** 10 to 12 minutes, or until liver is tender. Top with reserved bacon. Serve, if desired, over rice.

BURGUNDY BEEF

6 slices bacon, cut crosswise into sixths
2 medium onions, cut into chunks
½ pound fresh mushrooms, sliced
3 medium carrots, cut ¼ inch thick
1 clove garlic, finely chopped
2 pounds boneless beef, cut into 1-inch pieces
1 can (10½ oz.) condensed golden mushroom soup
1 cup Burgundy wine
1 tablespoon Worcestershire sauce
1 teaspoon browning sauce
1 bay leaf
½ teaspoon basil, crushed
½ teaspoon salt
¼ teaspoon pepper

Yield: 8 Servings

Cook bacon in 3-quart casserole, at **HIGH** 6 to 6½ minutes. Stir once. Remove bacon; reserve. Remove all but 2 tablespoons drippings. To dish, add onions, mushrooms, carrots and garlic. Stir to coat. Cook at **HIGH** 4 minutes. Add remaining ingredients; stir.

TO COOK BY TEMPERATURE: Insert temperature probe into liquid. Cover with lid. Set Insta-Matic **TEMP 8**. After selected temperature is reached, oven will automatically hold at 190°F for 2½ hours. Stir occasionally. At end of cooking time, stir in bacon. Remove bay leaf before serving.

TO COOK BY TIME: Cover with lid. Cook at **MEDIUM-LOW** 1 hour and at **LOW** 1½ hours. Stir occasionally. At end of cooking time, stir in bacon. Remove bay leaf before serving.

BRAISED BRISKET

3 to 3¼ pound beef brisket
1 cup water
1 envelope (1⅜ oz.) onion soup mix
1 regular size (10"×16") oven cooking bag*

Yield: 8 Servings

Prepare cooking bag according to package directions. Place brisket, water and soup mix in bag. Set in 12×8-inch dish. Close bag with nylon tie or cotton string. Make 6 (½-in.) slits in top of bag. Cook at **HIGH** 5 minutes and at **LOW** 90 minutes, or until beef is tender. Let stand 10 minutes before serving.

*****Note:** Brisket may also be cooked in covered casserole dish.*

MARVELOUS MEAT LOAF

1½ pounds ground beef
1 egg
½ cup dry bread crumbs
⅓ cup catsup
⅓ cup finely chopped onion
2 tablespoons milk or water
1 teaspoon Worcestershire sauce
½ teaspoon salt
¼ teaspoon pepper

Yield: 6 Servings

Combine all ingredients. In 12×8-inch dish, shape beef mixture into loaf (about 8″×4″).

TO COOK BY TEMPERATURE: Center Temp Probe in meat loaf. Cover with wax paper. Set Programmable Temp at **MEDIUM**, 150°F.

TO COOK BY TIME: Cook at **MEDIUM** 20 to 24 minutes.

TO COMPLETE: Drain liquid occasionally. If necessary, shield ends of loaf with aluminum foil halfway through cooking. Let stand, covered, 5 minutes before serving.

Hint: While meat loaf is standing, heat 1 cup gravy or seasoned tomato sauce; pour over loaf before serving, if desired.

MIDGET MEAT LOAF I-M

1 pound ground beef
1 egg
⅓ cup dry bread crumbs
⅓ cup catsup
2 tablespoons milk or water
2 envelopes (¼ oz. ea.) instant onion soup

Yield: 4 Servings

Combine all ingredients. In 8-inch square dish, shape beef mixture into loaf.

TO COOK BY INSTA-MATIC: Cover completely with plastic wrap; cook on **COOK 2**. After cooking, release plastic wrap.

TO COOK BY TIME: Cook at **MEDIUM** 14 to 16 minutes.

TO COMPLETE: Drain liquid occasionally. If necessary, shield ends of loaf with aluminum foil halfway through cooking. Let stand, covered, 5 minutes before serving.

Hint: For even quicker cooking, shape meat into ring shape in 9-inch pie plate. Cook 9 to 10 minutes.

Note: For TWO Servings, *follow above procedure using ½ pound ground beef, 1 egg, ¼ cup bread crumbs, 2 tablespoons catsup and 1 envelope instant onion soup. Shape into two loaves. Cook 7 to 8 minutes.*

STUFFED GREEN PEPPERS

1 pound ground beef
1 medium onion, finely chopped
2 cans (8 oz. ea.) tomato sauce, divided
¼ cup water
3 tablespoons Parmesan cheese, divided
1 teaspoon salt
⅛ teaspoon pepper
½ cup instant rice
4 medium green peppers (about 1 lb.)

Yield: 4 Servings

Crumble ground beef in medium glass bowl. Stir in onion. Cook at **HIGH** 3½ to 4½ minutes, or until beef loses pink color. Stir once; drain. Stir in 1 can tomato sauce, water, 1 tablespoon cheese, salt and pepper. Cook, covered with plastic wrap, at **HIGH** 2½ to 3½ minutes. Stir in rice. Let stand, covered, 5 minutes.
Cut peppers in half lengthwise; remove seeds and rinse. Spoon beef-rice filling into each half; place in 12×8-inch dish. Top with remaining sauce and cheese. Cover with plastic wrap. Cook at **HIGH** 10 to 12 minutes, or until peppers are tender. Let stand, covered, 5 minutes before serving.

STUFFED MEAT LOAF **I-M**

1½ pounds lean ground beef
2 cans (8 oz.) tomato sauce, divided
1 egg
½ cup seasoned dry bread crumbs
¼ cup finely chopped green onion
2 tablespoons finely chopped celery
½ teaspoon salt
¼ teaspoon pepper
1 cup (4 oz.) shredded natural mozzarella cheese
2 thin slices boiled ham
2 tablespoons chopped stuffed green olives

Yield: 6 Servings

In medium bowl, combine meat, 1 can tomato sauce, egg, bread crumbs, green onion, celery, salt and peper; mix well.
In 12×8-inch dish, shape one-half of meat mixture into an 8×5-inch rectangle. Top with cheese, ham and olives. Spread remaining meat mixture over cheese, ham and olives. Seal edges all around. Pour remaining can of tomato sauce over meat.

TO COOK BY INSTA-MATIC: Cover completely with plastic wrap; cook on **COOK 2**. After cooking, release plastic wrap.

TO COOK BY TIME: Cover with wax paper. Cook at **HIGH** 8 minutes and **MEDIUM-LOW** 15 minutes.

TO COMPETE: Let stand, covered, 5 minutes before serving.

CHEESEBURGER PIE

1 pound ground beef
1 package (5 oz.) instant mashed potato
  flakes (2¼ cups), divided
1¼ cups milk, divided
1 egg
¼ cup catsup
1 tablespoon dried onion flakes
1½ teaspoons salt, divided
¼ teaspoon pepper, divided
6 slices American cheese, divided
1 cup hot water
2 tablespoons butter or margarine

Yield: 4 Servings

Combine ground beef, 1⅓ cups instant mashed potato flakes, 1 cup milk, egg, catsup, onion, 1 teaspoon salt and ⅛ teaspoon pepper. Spread into 9-inch pie plate. Cook at **MEDIUM-HIGH** 6½ to 7½ minutes; drain. Arrange 2 slices cheese on top. Let stand, loosely covered, 7 minutes. Meanwhile, in medium glass bowl, combine water, butter, remaining milk, salt and pepper. Cook at **MEDIUM-HIGH** 5 to 6 minutes. Add remaining instant mashed potato flakes and cheese, diced; stir until potatoes are fluffy. Spread potato mixture over "cheeseburger". Cook at **MEDIUM-HIGH** 2 to 3 minutes or until heated through.

SALISBURY STEAK

1 can (4 oz.) sliced mushrooms, drained
1½ pounds ground beef
1 can (10¾ oz.) condensed golden
  mushroom soup, divided
1 egg
¼ cup milk
½ cup dry bread crumbs
1 small onion, finely chopped
⅛ teaspoon pepper

Yield: 6 Servings

Chop half of mushrooms. Combine chopped mushrooms, ground beef, ¼ can of soup and remaining ingredients. Shape into 6 patties and arrange in 12×8-inch dish. Cook, covered with wax paper, at **MEDIUM-HIGH** 8 to 10 minutes; drain. Combine remaining soup and mushrooms. Pour over patties. Cook, covered with wax paper, 3 to 4 minutes. Let stand, covered, 5 minutes before serving.

PIZZA WHEELS

1 pound ground beef
2 tablespoons finely chopped onion
½ teaspoon salt
Oregano
¼ cup spaghetti sauce
4 slices mozzarella cheese, cut into strips

Yield: 4 Servings

Combine ground beef, onion, salt and ¼ teaspoon oregano. Shape into 4 patties raising the edge ¼ inch to form a center well. Arrange patties in 8-inch square dish. Cook at **MEDIUM-HIGH** 3 to 4 minutes; drain. Fill center well with spaghetti sauce and sprinkle with oregano. Cook at **MEDIUM-HIGH** 1 to 1½ minutes. Top with cheese and let stand, covered, 3 minutes before serving.

Note: For TWO Servings, follow above procedure; halve all ingredients. Cook patties 1½ to 2 minutes and with sauce ½ to 1 minute.

SWEDISH MEATBALLS ⬛I-M

1 pound lean ground beef
1 egg
½ cup dry bread crumbs
½ cup milk, divided
1 small onion, finely chopped
2 teaspoons parsley flakes
½ teaspoon salt
⅛ teaspoon allspice
⅛ teaspoon pepper
1 can (10¾ oz.) condensed cream of
  mushroom soup

Yield: 4–6 Servings

Combine ground beef, egg, bread crumbs, ¼ cup milk, onion, parsley, salt, allspice and pepper. Shape into 1¼-inch meatballs (about 30) and arrange in 12×8-inch baking dish.

TO COOK BY INSTA-MATIC: Cover completely with plastic wrap. Cook on **COOK 7**. After time appears in display window, stir once.

TO COOK BY TIME: Cook at **MEDIUM** for 9 to 10 minutes. Stir once, halfway through cooking time.

TO COMPLETE: Blend soup with remaining milk. Pour over meatballs. Stir lightly to coat. Cook, covered, 4 minutes or until heated through. Serve over buttered noodles sprinkled with chopped parsley, if desired.

SAVORY CABBAGE ROLLS

1 small head cabbage
1 pound ground beef
2 medium onions, finely chopped
1 can (15 oz.) tomato sauce, divided
½ cup cooked rice (see chart, page 188)
1 teaspoon salt
⅛ teaspoon pepper
2 tablespoons packed brown sugar
2 tablespoons cider vinegar

Yield: 4 Servings

Cut core from cabbage; rinse. In medium glass bowl, cook, covered with plastic wrap, at **HIGH** 4 to 5 minutes. Remove 10 leaves; cut out hard center rib from each leaf (make a V-shape cut). Use remaining cabbage in other recipes. Into medium bowl, crumble ground beef and combine with onions, ½ tomato sauce, rice, salt and pepper. To stuff cabbage, place beef-rice filling in cabbage leaf; roll up, folding edges in. Arrange seam-side down in 12×8-inch dish. Blend remaining tomato sauce with brown sugar and vinegar. Pour over rolls. Cover with plastic wrap. Cook at **MEDIUM** 28 to 30 minutes. Let stand, covered, 5 minutes before serving.

ITALIAN MEATBALLS

1 pound ground beef
1 egg
1½ cups soft bread crumbs
¼ cup water or milk
2 to 3 tablespoons grated Parmesan
  cheese
¾ teaspoon oregano
1 teaspoon parsley
1 teaspoon onion salt

Yield: 4 Servings

Combine all ingredients and shape into 1½-inch meatballs (about 20). Arrange in 12×8-inch dish. Cook at **MEDIUM-HIGH** 7½ to 8½ minutes; drain. Let stand, 3 minutes before serving.

ORIENTAL PEPPER BURGERS

1 pound lean ground beef
¼ teaspoon salt
⅛ teaspoon pepper
1 medium onion, sliced
1 medium green pepper, cut into chunks
1 can (8 oz.) tomato sauce
¼ teaspoon ginger
4 teaspoons soy sauce

Yield: 4 Servings

Combine beef, salt and pepper; shape into 4 patties and arrange in 8-inch square dish. Cover with wax paper. Cook at **MEDIUM-HIGH** 4 to 5 minutes; drain. Top patties with onion and green pepper. Combine tomato sauce, ginger and soy sauce; pour over top.
Cook, covered with wax paper, at **MEDIUM-HIGH** 5½ to 6½ minutes, or until vegetables are tender. Let stand, covered, 5 minutes before serving.

VEAL PAPRIKA I-M

1 pound boneless veal, cut into 1½-inch cubes
½ pound fresh mushrooms, sliced
1 cup chicken broth, divided
1 large onion finely chopped
1 teaspoon paprika
½ teaspoon salt
⅛ to ¼ teaspoon pepper
Dash caraway seeds
3 tablespoons flour
½ cup sour cream

Yield: 4 Servings

In 2-quart casserole, combine veal, mushrooms, ½ cup broth, onion, paprika, salt, pepper and caraway. Cover with lid.

TO COOK BY INSTA-MATIC: Cook on **COOK 2**. After time appears in display window, stir occasionally.

TO COOK BY TIME: Cook at **HIGH** 7 minutes and at **MEDIUM-LOW** 21 minutes; stir occasionally.

TO COMPLETE: Blend flour with remaining ½ cup broth until smooth. Stir into dish. Cook at **HIGH** 2 to 3 minutes, or until sauce is thickened. Blend in sour cream.

VEAL CUTLETS CORDON BLEU

4 veal cutlets (about 1 lb.), pounded thin*
2 thin slices cooked ham, halved
2 slices (rectangular) Swiss cheese, halved
1 cup seasoned dry bread crumbs
½ teaspoon salt
⅛ teaspoon pepper
Dash allspice
1 egg, beaten with ¼ cup water
3 tablespoons oil

Yield: 4 Servings

On one side of each cutlet, place ham and cheese; fold cutlet in half. Pound edges together to seal or secure with wooden toothpicks. Dip cutlets in bread crumbs mixed with salt, pepper and allspice; dip in egg, then again in bread crumbs. Coat bottom of 12×8-inch dish with half of oil; place cutlets in dish. Sprinkle remaining oil on cutlets. Cook at **MEDIUM-HIGH** 7 to 8 minutes turning cutlets over once. Let stand, covered, with wax paper, 5 minutes before serving.

Variation: *Use chicken cutlets for veal.*

WURST MIT KRAUT

6 tablespoons butter or margarine
1½ cups chopped onion (about 2 medium)
2 cups sliced apples (about 2 medium)
2 cans (16 oz. ea.) sauerkraut, drained and rinsed
½ cup beef broth
¼ teaspoon caraway seeds
¼ teaspoon pepper
6 knockwurst sausages (about 3 oz. ea.)

Yield: 6 Servings

In 12×8-inch dish, combine butter and onion. Cook at **HIGH** 3 to 3½ minutes. Stir in apples. Cook at **HIGH** 3 to 4½ minutes. Stir in sauerkraut, broth, caraway and pepper.
Score knockwurst diagonally and arrange on sauerkraut mixture. Cook at **HIGH** 8 to 9 minutes. Rearrange knockwurst once. Let stand, covered, 5 minutes.

APPLE STUFFED PORK CHOPS

4 pork chops, 1-inch thick **I-M**
¼ cup butter or margarine, melted
½ cup chopped apple
½ cup herb seasoned stuffing mix
¼ cup (1 oz.) shredded Cheddar cheese
2 tablespoons chopped celery
1 tablespoon chopped onion
1 tablespoon chopped raisins
2 tablespoons orange juice
¼ teaspoon salt
1 tablespoon Worcestershire sauce
1 tablespoon water

Yield: 4 Servings

Cut a horizontal slit in each pork chop to form pocket. In small mixing bowl, combine butter, apple, stuffing mix, cheese, celery, onion, raisins, orange juice and salt; mix well. Fill each pocket with stuffing mix. Secure opening with wooden toothpicks*. Arrange pork chops in 12×8-inch dish. Mix Worcestershire with water and brush on pork chops.

TO COOK BY INSTA-MATIC: Cover completely with plastic wrap. Cook on **COOK 6**. After cooking, release plastic wrap.

TO COOK BY TIME: Cover with wax paper. Cook at **MEDIUM** 17 minutes.

TO COMPLETE: Let stand, covered, 5 minutes. Meanwhile, place remainder of stuffing in a small microwave safe bowl. Cover with plastic wrap. Cook at **MEDIUM** 2 to 3 minutes, or until hot.

__Note:__ Break toothpicks in half, otherwise they may poke through plastic.

CHINESE PORK AND GREEN VEGETABLES

2 tablespoons oil
1 pound boneless pork, cut into thin strips
2 tablespoons soy sauce
⅛ teaspoon garlic powder
1 package (6 oz.) frozen pea pods, defrosted (see page 35)
2 bunches green onions, cut into ¾-inch pieces (about ⅔ cup)
1½ to 2 tablespoons cornstarch
1 cup beef broth

Yield: 4 Servings

Heat oil in 12×8-inch dish at **MEDIUM-HIGH** 2 minutes. Stir in pork, soy sauce and garlic. Cook at **MEDIUM-HIGH** 4 to 5 minutes; stir occasionally. Add pea pods and green onions. Cook, covered with plastic wrap, at **MEDIUM-HIGH** 3 minutes; stir once.
Blend cornstarch with broth until smooth. Stir into pork. Cook at **MEDIUM-HIGH** 3 to 4 minutes, or until sauce is slightly thickened. Stir occasionally. Serve, if desired, over rice.

FRUITED GLAZED HAM

⅓ cup packed light brown sugar
¼ cup light corn syrup
2 tablespoons prepared mustard
10 pound ham, bone-in, cooked
Whole cloves
1 can (20 oz.) sliced pineapple, drained
8 to 10 maraschino cherries

Yield: 12–14 Servings

In small glass bowl, combine sugar, syrup and mustard; set aside. In 12×8-inch dish, place ham fat-side down on microwave roasting rack. Shield ham by wrapping a 3-inch wide strip of foil around large end of ham. Secure foil to ham with wooden toothpicks. Fold 1½-inches over cut surface. For shank ham halves, shield shank bone by cupping it with foil. Cook, covered with wax paper, at **MEDIUM-LOW** 30 minutes. Remove skin from ham and score fat. Place fat-side up on rack set in 12×8-inch dish. Reshield ham as directed above. Cook at **MEDIUM-LOW** 30 minutes; set aside. Cook glaze at **MEDIUM**, 3 minutes or until sugar is dissolved and mixture boils; stir once. Brush ham with glaze; reshield.

TO COOK BY TEMPERATURE: Insert probe into center of ham, not touching bone, fat or foil. Set Programmable Temp at **MEDIUM-LOW** 100°F and **LOW** 120°F. When temperature in display window reaches 100°F, remove foil. Drain liquid from dish. Arrange cloves and fruit on ham. Brush ham and fruit with glaze. Continue cooking.

TO COOK BY TIME: Cook at **MEDIUM-LOW** for 10 minutes. Remove foil. Drain liquid from dish. Arrange cloves and fruit on ham. Brush ham and fruit with glaze. Continue cooking an additional 15 to 20 minutes, or until ham registers 120°F when tested with a conventional meat thermometer. (Remove ham from oven before reading thermometer.)

TO COMPLETE: Let stand, covered, 15 minutes before serving.

PEACHY PORK ROAST

Water
1 can (8½ oz.) sliced peaches, drained and chopped; reserve syrup
1 package (6 oz.) stuffing mix for pork with seasoning packet
1 egg
⅓ cup chopped walnuts
¼ cup butter or margarine
3 to 3¼ pound pork rib roast (about 6 ribs)*
¼ cup peach preserves

Yield: 6 Servings

In 2-cup glass measure, add enough water to reserved syrup to equal 1½ to 1¾ cups. Cook at **HIGH** 2 to 3 minutes or until hot. In medium bowl, combine liquid with peaches, stuffing mix (and included seasoning packet), egg, walnuts and butter. Stir until liquid is absorbed and butter is melted.
Cut pockets in pork roast, one opposite each bone. Stuff each pocket with 2 tablespoons stuffing. Secure with cotton string or wooden toothpicks. Place roast fat-side-down on microwave roasting rack set in 12×8-inch dish.

TO COOK BY TEMPERATURE: Insert probe into roast making sure tip of probe is touching meat, not stuffing. Set Insta-Matic **TEMP 6** or Programmable Temp at **MEDIUM-LOW** 100°F and **LOW** 170°F. When temperature in display window reaches 100°F, remove probe from roast without disconnecting from oven. Turn roast fat-side up. Reinsert probe into a new hole. Continue cooking. When temperature in display window reaches 140°F, brush on peach preserves.

TO COOK BY TIME: Cook at **MEDIUM-LOW** 12 to 13½ minutes per pound. Halfway through cooking, turn roast fat-side up. Baste occasionally, with preserves.

TO COMPLETE: Let stand, covered, 10 minutes before serving. Meanwhile, at **MEDIUM-LOW** cook remaining stuffing 6 to 7 minutes; stir twice. Serve with roast. To carve roast, remove string; cut in between each bone.

*****Hint:** *For easy carving, when buying roast, have the backbone (chine bone) cracked.*

POLISH SAUSAGE (KIELBASA) WITH RED CABBAGE

1 small head (about 2 lb.) red cabbage, shredded*
1 small apple, chopped
¼ cup sugar
¼ cup cider vinegar
1 tablespoon dried onion flakes
½ teaspoon caraway seeds
½ teaspoon salt
1 ring (1¾ to 2 lb.) Kielbasa sausage

Yield: 6 Servings

In 12×8-inch dish, combine cabbage, apple, sugar, vinegar, onion, caraway and salt. Cook, covered with plastic wrap, at **HIGH** 7 to 8 minutes; stir twice.
Meanwhile, make ¼-inch slits every few inches in Kielbasa; arrange on red cabbage. Cook, covered with plastic wrap, at **HIGH** 12 to 13 minutes, or until heated through. Let stand, covered, 5 minutes before serving.

Substitution: Use 2 jars (16 oz ea.) red cabbage, drained for fresh cabbage. Do not cook cabbage separately. Arrange Kielbasa on red cabbage blended with remaining ingredients. Cook covered, 15 to 17 minutes or until heated through.

SWEET 'N SOUR PORK

1 can (8¼ oz.) chunk pineapple in heavy syrup, drained; reserve ⅓ cup syrup
¼ cup cider vinegar
1 tablespoon cornstarch
2 tablespoons oil
1 pound boneless pork, cut into ¾-inch cubes
¼ cup soy sauce
1 bunch green onions, thinly sliced (about 3 tbsp.)
1 green pepper, cut into small chunks

Yield: 4 Servings

In small glass bowl, combine reserved syrup, vinegar and cornstarch. Cook at **MEDIUM-HIGH** ¾ to 1 minute, or until thickened; stir once.
Heat oil in 8-inch square dish at **MEDIUM-HIGH** 2 minutes. Stir in pork, soy sauce and onions. Cook at **MEDIUM-HIGH** 7 to 8 minutes; stir twice. Add green pepper and pineapple. Cook, covered with plastic wrap, at **MEDIUM-HIGH** 2 to 3 minutes, or until pork is tender. Stir in sauce and let stand, covered, 5 minutes before serving.

CRANBERRY GLAZED HAM

¾ cup cranberry juice
¼ cup orange juice
¼ cup packed brown sugar
¼ cup raisins
1 tablespoon cornstarch
Dash cloves
Whole cloves
3 to 5 pound canned ham

Yield: 12–20 Servings

In small glass bowl, combine juices, sugar, raisins, cornstarch and ground cloves. Cook at **HIGH** 2½ to 3½ minutes, or until glaze is thickened; stir twice. Set aside. Decorate ham with whole cloves. Place ham in 12×8-inch dish.

TO COOK BY TEMPERATURE: Insert probe into center of ham, not touching bone or fat. Set Programmable Temp at **MEDIUM-LOW** 100°F and **LOW** 120°F. After 20 minutes, shield top cut-edge of ham with a 1½-inch strip of foil. Wrap strip of foil around ham; secure to body of ham with wooden toothpicks. Fold 1-inch over cut surface, being careful to avoid touching probe. When temperature in display window reaches 100°F, remove foil and glaze ham.

TO COOK BY TIME: Cook at **MEDIUM-LOW** for 9 to 10 minutes per pound. After 20 minutes, shield top cut-edge of ham with a 1½-inch strip of foil. Wrap strip of foil around ham; secure to body of ham with wooden toothpicks. Fold 1-inch over cut surface. When ham registers 100°F when tested with a conventional meat thermometer, (remove ham from oven before reading thermometer) remove foil and glaze ham. Continue cooking.

TO COMPLETE: Let stand, covered, 10 minutes before serving.

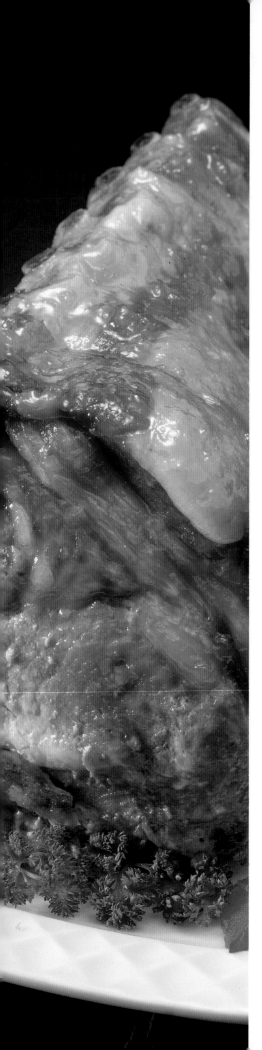

APRICOT GLAZED PORK ROAST

1 jar (12 oz.) apricot preserves
½ teaspoon ginger
1 tablespoon lemon juice
4 to 5 pound pork rib roast*
Pepper

Yield: 6–8 Servings

In small glass bowl, combine preserves, ginger and lemon juice. Cook at **HIGH** to 2 minutes or until hot. Season roast with pepper. Place roast fat-side down on microwave roasting rack set in 12×8-inch dish. During cooking, baste roast with glaze three times.

TO COOK BY TEMPERATURE: Insert probe into center of roast. Set Insta-Matic **TEMP 6** or Programmable Temp at **MEDIUM-LOW** 100°F and **LOW** 170°F. When temperature in display window reaches 100°F, remove probe from roast without disconnecting from oven. Turn roast fat-side up. Reinsert probe in a new hole. Continue cooking. Occasionally drain liquid.

TO COOK BY TIME: Cook at **MEDIUM-LOW** 12 to 13½ minutes per pound, or until roast registers 170°F when tested with a conventional meat thermometer. (Remove roast from microwave oven before reading the temperature.) Halfway through cooking, turn roast fat-side up. Occasionally drain liquid.

TO COMPLETE: Let stand, covered, 15 minutes before carving.

***Hint:** For easy carving, when buying a roast, have the backbone (chine bone) cracked.*

SOUTHERN BARBECUED RIBS

2 pounds pork backribs or spareribs, cut into individual ribs
1 cup barbecue sauce
2 tablespoons honey or dark corn syrup
2 tablespoons flour
1 tablespoon soy sauce

Yield: 4 Servings

Arrange ribs, meaty-side down in 12×8-inch dish. Combine remaining ingredients; pour over ribs. Cover with wax paper. Cook at **HIGH** 10 minutes and at **MEDIUM-LOW** 25 to 30 minutes, or until ribs are tender. Halfway through cooking, turn ribs over; rearrange. Spoon sauce over ribs.

MINT GLAZED LAMB

4 to 5 pound leg of lamb
3 cloves garlic
1 teaspoon crushed rosemary
¼ teaspoon pepper
½ cup mint jelly
1 can (8½ oz.) pear slices, drained and mashed; reserve 1 tablespoon syrup

Yield: about 8 Servings

Make 6 slits in lamb, insert ⅓ clove garlic in each. Mix rosemary and pepper; rub over lamb. Place lamb on microwave roasting rack set in 12×8-inch dish. In small glass bowl, combine remaining garlic, finely chopped, jelly and reserved syrup. Cook at **MEDIUM** 2 to 3 minutes or until melted. Stir in pears. Spoon ⅓ mint glaze over lamb.

TO COOK BY TEMPERATURE: Insert temperature probe into meaty portion of lamb not touching bone. Set Insta-Matic TEMP or Programmable Temp according to desired doneness of meat; see roasting chart on page 83. When temperature in display reaches 100°F, remove probe from meat without disconnecting from oven wall. Turn roast oven and reinsert probe. Brush with remaining mint glaze. Drain liquid occasionally. Continue cooking until meat reaches selected temperature.

TO COOK BY TIME: Cook at **MEDIUM-LOW**; see roasting chart on page 83 to determine minutes per pound for desired degree of doneness. Turn meat over halfway through cooking. Brush with remaining mint glaze and drain liquid occasionally.

TO COMPLETE: Let stand, covered, 15 minutes before serving.

PERSIAN LAMB WITH PEACHES

Water
1 can (16 oz.) peach slices, drained (reserve syrup)
1½ pounds boneless lamb, cut into 1½-inch cubes*
1 envelope (1 oz.) onion-mushroom soup mix
1 tablespoon lemon juice
¼ teaspoon cinnamon
⅛ teaspoon cloves
2 tablespoons cornstarch
¼ cup raisins

Yield: 6 Servings

Add enough water to reserved syrup to equal 1 cup. In 2-quart casserole, combine syrup, lamb, soup mix, lemon juice, cinnamon and cloves. Cover with lid. Cook at **HIGH** 6 to 7 minutes and at **LOW** 30 minutes or until lamb is tender. Stir twice. Blend cornstarch with ¼ cup water until smooth. Stir in cornstarch, peaches and raisins. Cook at **HIGH** 4 to 5 minutes, or until sauce is thickened. Stir once.

***Substitution:** Use beef cubes for lamb.*

103

CROWN ROAST OF LAMB

1 package (6 oz.) long grain and wild rice
1 small onion, chopped
¼ cup sliced celery
¼ cup sliced natural almonds
2 tablespoons butter or margarine
2 small oranges, peeled, sectioned and
  chopped
¼ cup orange marmalade
Browning sauce
3 pound crown roast of lamb

Yield: 6 Servings

Prepare rice according to package directions, omitting butter. (See page 188 for microwave cooking instructions.) In medium glass bowl, cook celery, onion, almonds and butter 3 to 4 minutes at **HIGH**, or until vegetables are tender crisp. Stir vegetables and oranges into the rice; set aside.

Heat marmalade in small glass bowl at **MEDIUM** 1 minute, or until melted. Brush inside and outside of roast with browning sauce, then marmalade. Set roast on microwave roasting rack set in 12×8-inch dish. Cover with wax paper.

TO COOK BY TEMPERATURE: Insert probe into meaty portion of roast, making sure tip of probe is not touching bone or fat. Cook on Insta-Matic Temp or Programmable Temp according to desired doneness of meat; see roasting chart on page 83.

TO COOK BY TIME: Cook at **MEDIUM-LOW** 20 to 22 minutes for medium, 28 to 30 minutes for well, or until roast registers 130°F or 170°F when tested with a conventional meat thermometer. (Remove roast from oven before reading temperature.).

TO COMPLETE: After cooking, transfer roast to serving platter. Let stand, covered. Reheat stuffing mixture at **HIGH** for 2 to 3 minutes, or until hot. Fill center of roast with stuffing mixture. Let stand, covered, 5 minutes before serving.

CURRY LAMB

1 small onion, finely chopped
¼ cup butter or margarine
3 tablespoons flour
1 pound boneless lamb, cut into 1½-inch
  cubes
1 can (10¾ oz.) chicken broth
⅓ cup raisins
⅓ cup peanuts
3 tablespoons lemon juice
1 tablespoon curry powder
½ teaspoon ginger
½ teaspoon salt
½ cup flaked coconut
2 cups cooked rice (see page 188)

Yield: 4 Servings

Cook onion and butter in 2-quart casserole at **HIGH** 5 to 6 minutes, stir once. Stir flour, then lamb, broth, raisins, peanuts, lemon juice, curry powder, ginger and salt. Cook covered with lid, at **HIGH** 5 minutes and **LOW**, 20 to 25 minutes or until lamb is tender; stir twice. Sprinkle with coconut. Let stand, covered, 5 mintues before serving over hot rice.

POULTRY

Roast turkey is not only for special holidays! The long preparation once associated with cooking poultry vanishes when you microwave this family favorite. All types of poultry can be easily cooked in microwave minutes. You will please everyone with delicious moist meals while saving yourself lots of time and effort.

GENERAL DIRECTIONS FOR ROASTING WHOLE POULTRY

Season as desired, but salt after cooking. Browning sauce mixed with equal parts of butter will enhance the appearance.

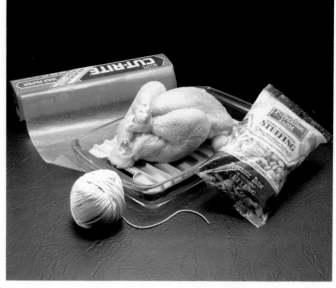

Poultry may be stuffed or unstuffed. Tie legs with cotton string. Place poultry on microwave roasting rack in a 12×8-inch dish. Poultry over 4 pounds should be placed breast-side down on rack and turned over halfway through cooking. Cover loosely with wax paper to prevent spatter.

During cooking it may be necessary to shield legs, wings and the breast bone to prevent overcooking. Wooden toothpicks can be used to hold small strips of foil in place.

If a large amount of juice accumulates in baking dish, drain occasionally. If desired, reserve for making gravy.

DIRECTIONS FOR ROASTING WHOLE POULTRY

Less tender hens should be cooked in liquid such as soup or broth. Use ¼ cup per pound of poultry. Use an oven cooking bag or covered casserole. Select a covered casserole deep enough so that hen does not touch the lid.

If an oven cooking bag is used, prepare bag according to package directions. Do not use wire or metal twist-ties to close bag. Use nylon ties provided, otherwise use a piece of cotton string or a strip cut from the open end of the bag. Make six ½-inch slits in top of bag to allow steam to escape.

To Cook by Time:
Multiply the weight of the poultry by the minimum number of minutes per pound recommended in chart on page 109.

To Cook by Temperature Probe:
Place turkey or chicken over 4 pounds breast-side down on microwave rack set in a 12×8-inch dish.
Cook chicken and turkeys four minutes per pound at MEDIUM.

Turn poultry breast-side up. Insert probe parallel to the leg into the thickest portion of the thigh. The probe should be between the inner thigh and body of the bird and should not touch bones.
Cook on Insta-Matic Temperature or Programmable Temperature as indicated in charts or recipes. Probe Cooking is not recommended for poultry weighing less than 4 pounds. It is too difficult to accurately position probe in smaller size poultry.

After cooking, check the temperature of large chickens and turkeys with a meat thermometer. Check the temperature in both thigh muscles. If thermometer touches bone, the reading may be inaccurate. Small chickens and game birds are cooked when juices run clear and drumstick readily moves up and down. If poultry is undercooked, cook a few more minutes at the recommended power level. Let stand, tented with foil, 10 to 15 minutes before carving.

POULTRY ROASTING CHART FOR TIME COOKING

POULTRY	POWER	APPROX. COOKING TIME (minutes per pound)	APPROX. TEMPERATURE AFTER STANDING
Cornish Hens	HIGH	7½ to 8½	————
Chickens (up to 3 lb.)	HIGH	7½ to 8½	————
Chickens (3 to 7 lb.)	MEDIUM	10 to 11½	180° to 190°F
Turkey (See page 121)	MEDIUM MEDIUM-LOW	4 to 5 5 to 6	180° to 190°F
Turkey Parts	MEDIUM	9½ to 11½	180° to 190°F
Goose	MEDIUM	9½ to 10½	180° to 190°F
Duck	MEDIUM	9½ to 10½	180° to 190°F
Pheasant	MEDIUM	8 to 9½	————

POULTRY ROASTING CHART FOR TEMPERATURE PROBE

POULTRY	BREAST-SIDE DOWN		PROGRAMMABLE TEMP			
			INSTA-MATIC TEMP	BREAST-SIDE UP		APPROX. TEMPERATURE AFTER
	POWER	MINUTES PER POUND	SETTING	FIRST STAGE POWER & TEMP	SECOND STAGE POWER & TEMP	STANDING
Chicken (4 to 7 lb.)	MEDIUM	4 to 5	TEMP 7	MEDIUM 140°F →	MEDIUM-LOW 190°F	180° to 190°F
Turkey	MEDIUM	4 to 5	TEMP 7	MEDIUM 140°F →	MEDIUM-LOW 190°F	180° to 190°F

DIRECTIONS FOR COOKING POULTRY PIECES

Arrange pieces skin-side up, with meatier portions toward edge of the dish.

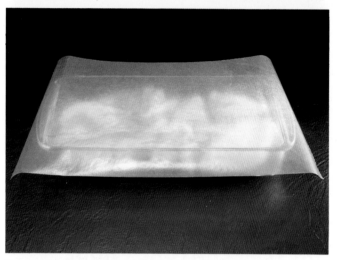

To Cook by Time: Cover with wax paper, multiply the weight by 5½ to 6 minutes per pound. Cook at HIGH.

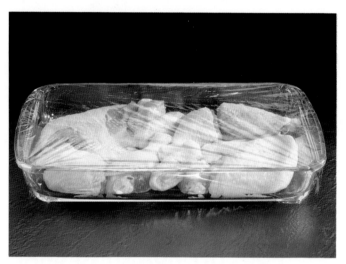

To Cook by Insta-Matic: Cover completely with plastic wrap and cook on COOK 4.

Poultry is cooked when juices are clear (no pink color). If there is a slight pink color in the juice, return poultry parts to the oven and cook one or two minutes longer.

Let stand 5 minutes before serving or as recipe indicates.

CHICKEN CACCIATORE I-M

2½ to 3 pound chicken, cut into serving pieces
1 can (15 oz.) tomato sauce
1 jar (4½ oz.) sliced mushrooms, drained
½ cup chopped onion
1 tablespoon sugar, optional
1 teaspoon oregano
1 teaspoon salt
1 clove garlic, finely chopped
¼ teaspoon pepper

Yield: 4 Servings

Arrange chicken in 12×8-inch dish with meatier portions toward edge of dish. Combine remaining ingredients, pour over chicken.

TO COOK BY INSTA-MATIC: Cover completely with plastic wrap. Cook on **COOK 2**. After time appears in display window, turn chicken pieces over and rearrange. After cooking, release plastic wrap.

TO COOK BY TIME: Cover with wax paper. Cook at **HIGH** 18 to 20 minutes. Halfway through cooking time turn chicken pieces over and rearrange.

TO COMPLETE: Chicken should be tender. Let stand, covered, 5 minutes. Serve, if desired, with spaghetti.

BARBECUED CHICKEN

2½ to 3 pound chicken, cut into serving pieces
1 cup barbecue sauce*

Yield: 4 Servings

Arrange chicken in 12×8-inch dish with meatier portions toward edge of dish. Spread sauce evenly over chicken. Cover with wax paper. Cook at **HIGH** 10 to 13 minutes. Baste chicken with sauce. Cook, uncovered, at **HIGH** 3 to 5 minutes. Chicken should be tender. Let stand, covered, 5 minutes before serving.

__Hint:__ Use bottled barbecue sauce or see page 61 for tangy home made sauce.

CALIFORNIA CHICKEN I-M

2 chicken breasts, split (1¾ to 2 lb.)
2 teaspoons lemon juice
1 teaspoon dried onion flakes
Basil
Pepper
⅔ cup (2⅔ oz.) shredded Cheddar cheese
½ small avocado, thinly sliced
4 thin slices tomato

Yield: 4 Servings

Arrange chicken in 8-inch square dish with meatier portions toward edge of dish. Sprinkle with lemon juice, onion flakes, basil and pepper.

TO COOK BY INSTA-MATIC: Cover completely with plastic wrap. Cook on **COOK 4**. After time appears in display window, turn chicken pieces over.

TO COOK BY TIME: Cover with wax paper. Cook at **HIGH** 8½ to 9½ minutes, or until chicken is tender.

TO COMPLETE: Top chicken with ⅓ cup cheese, avocado, tomato and remaining cheese. Cook, covered, with wax paper at **HIGH** 2½ to 3 minutes. Let stand, covered, 5 minutes before serving.

*Note: **For TWO Servings,** follow above procedure; halve all ingredients. Cook chicken 6 to 6½ minutes and vegetables 1½ to 2 minutes. **For ONE Serving,** cook chicken 4 to 4½ minutes and vegetables ¾ to 1¼ minutes.*

IN-A-JAM KABOBS

⅓ cup orange marmalade
2 tablespoons orange juice
2 tablespoons soy sauce
½ teaspoon lemon juice
Dash ginger
2 boneless chicken breasts, skinned and cut into 1½-inch pieces (about 1 to 1¼ lb.)
1 package (10 oz.) frozen brussel sprouts, defrosted (see page 35)

Yield: 4 Servings

In medium glass bowl, combine marmalade, orange juice, soy sauce, lemon juice and ginger. Cook at **HIGH** 2½ to 3 minutes. Add chicken and marinate, if desired, 30 minutes.
On four 9 or 10-inch wooden skewers*, alternately thread chicken and brussel sprouts. Arrange skewers on 8-inch square baking dish. Cook at **HIGH** 5 to 6 minutes, or until chicken is tender. Rearrange skewers once and brush with marinade twice.

***Note:** If wooden skewers are unavailable, metal skewers may be used. Refer to page 9 for special instructions.*

CHICKEN LIVERS SUPREME

½ pound fresh mushrooms, sliced
⅓ cup chopped onion
¼ cup butter or margarine
1 pound chicken livers, halved
2 to 3 tablespoons flour
1 teaspoon salt
½ teaspoon pepper
½ teaspoon thyme
Cooked rice, optional (see page 188)

Yield: 4 Servings

In 2½-quart casserole, combine mushrooms, onion and butter. Cook, covered with lid, at **HIGH** 3 to 4 minutes, or until onion and mushrooms are tender; stir once. Stir in livers tossed with flour, salt, pepper and thyme. Cook, covered, at **HIGH** 2 minutes and at **MEDIUM** 5 to 6 minutes, or until liver is tender, stir twice. Serve, if desired, with rice.

MOROCCAN CHICKEN

2 cups hot water
1 cup rice
1 envelope (1 oz.) onion-mushroom soup
  mix, divided
½ cup raisins
½ teaspoon cinnamon, divided
2½ to 3 pound chicken, cut into serving
  pieces
1 cup plain yogurt

Yield: 4 Servings

In 12×8-inch dish, combine water, rice, ½
envelope soup mix, raisins and ¼ teaspoon
cinnamon. Cook, covered with plastic wrap;
at **HIGH** 5 minutes and at **MEDIUM-LOW** 13
to 15 minutes, or until rice is almost
tender, stir once. Arrange chicken on rice
with meatier portions toward edge of dish.
Sprinkle with remaining cinnamon. Cook,
covered with wax paper, at **HIGH** 12 to 14
minutes, or until chicken is tender.
Rearrange chicken and stir rice once.
Spoon yogurt over chicken. Let stand,
covered, 5 minutes. If necessary, reheat at
MEDIUM-LOW 1½ to 2 minutes before
serving.

APRICOT GLAZED CHICKEN

2½ to 3 pound chicken, cut into serving
  pieces
¾ cup apricot preserves
½ cup bottled red Russian dressing
2 envelopes (¼ oz. ea.) instant onion soup

Yield: 4 Servings

Arrange chicken in 12×8-inch dish with
meatier portions toward edge of dish.
Cook, covered with wax paper, at **HIGH** 9
to 10 minutes, or until chicken is almost
tender; drain. Combine remaining
ingredients and spoon over chicken. Cook
chicken, uncovered, at **MEDIUM** 5 to 5½
minutes, or until chicken is glazed. Let
stand 5 minutes before serving.

CHICKEN VERONIQUE

2½ to 3 pound chicken, cut into serving
  pieces
3 tablespoons butter or margarine
1 teaspoon browning sauce
3 tablespoons flour
½ cup milk or half'n half
¼ cup white wine
1 cup halved green grapes
Toasted slivered almonds (see page 235)

Yield: 4 Servings

Prepare Buttered Baked Chicken, below
using chicken, butter and browning sauce.
Remove chicken to serving platter. Drain
liquid, reserving ¾ cup. Blend flour with
milk until smooth. Into baking dish, stir
flour, wine, reserved liquid and grapes.
Cook at **MEDIUM** 3½ to 4½ minutes, or
until sauce is thickened; stir twice. Pour
sauce over chicken and garnish with
almonds.

BUTTERED BAKED CHICKEN I-M

2½ to 3 pound chicken, cut into serving
  pieces
3 tablespoons butter or margarine, melted
1 teaspoon browning sauce

Yield: 4 Servings

Arrange chicken in 12×8-inch dish with,
meatier portions toward edge of dish.
Combine butter and browning sauce.

TO COOK BY INSTA-MATIC: Brush all of
the butter sauce over chicken. Cover
completely with plastic wrap. Cook on
COOK 4. After cooking, release plastic
wrap.

TO COOK BY TIME: Brush half of butter
mixture over chicken. Cover with wax
paper. Cook at **HIGH** 11 to 13 minutes.
Halfway through cooking, brush remaining
butter mixture on chicken.

TO COMPLETE: Chicken should be tender.
Let stand, covered, 5 minutes before
serving.

*Note: **For TWO Servings,** follow above
procedure. Halve all ingredients and
cook 5½ to 6½ minutes.
For ONE Serving, cook chicken 3½
to 4½ minutes.*

FIESTA CHICKEN ROLL-UPS I-M

2 boneless chicken breasts, skinned, split
   and pounded thin (about 1 to 1¼ lb.)
Chili powder
Pepper
2 ounces Cheddar cheese, cut into quarters
¼ cup sliced green olives
¼ cup butter or margarine, melted
¾ cup crushed taco or corn chips
1 can (8 oz.) taco or seasoned tomato
   sauce

Yield: 4 Servings

Season one side of each chicken breast
with chili powder and pepper. Place one
stick of cheese on each breast. Sprinkle 1
tablespoon of olives down center. Fold
edges over to enclose filling. Secure with
wooden toothpicks. Carefully roll in melted
butter, then crushed corn chips. Arrange
seam-side down in 8-inch square dish.

TO COOK BY INSTA-MATIC: Cover
completely with plastic wrap. Cook on
COOK 4. After cooking, release plastic
wrap.

TO COOK BY TIME: Cover with wax paper.
Cook at **MEDIUM** 8 to 9 minutes, or until
chicken is tender.

TO COMPLETE: Let stand, covered, 5
minutes. Meanwhile, in small glass bowl,
cook taco sauce at **HIGH** 2 to 3 minutes, or
until hot. Serve over chicken.

FRUITED GLAZED CHICKEN

¼ cup peach or apricot preserves
¼ teaspoon browning sauce
2½ to 3 pound chicken, cut into serving
   pieces
1 package (10 oz.) frozen mixed fruit,
   defrost (see page 35)
1 tablespoon cornstarch
½ teaspoon lemon juice, optional
Dash ginger or cinnamon

Yield: 4 Servings

Combine preserves and browning sauce in
small glass bowl. Cook at **HIGH** ½ to 1
minute. Arrange chicken in 12×8-inch dish
with meatier portions toward edge of dish.
Brush with ½ preserves. Cook, covered,
with wax paper, at **HIGH** 12 to 13 minutes.
Brush with remaining preserves halfway
through cooking. Remove chicken to
serving platter. Let stand, covered, 5
minutes.
Drain liquid, reserving ½ cup. In baking
dish, combine reserved liquid and
remaining ingredients. Cook at **HIGH** 3 to 4
minutes, or until sauce is slightly
thickened; stir twice. Serve over chicken.

TENDER CRISPY CHICKEN

8 small chicken pieces (about 2 lb.)
1 package (2⅜ oz.) seasoned coating mix
   for chicken

Yield: 4 Servings

Coat chicken according to package
directions. Arrange in 12×8-inch dish with
meatier portions toward edge of dish.
Cover with wax paper. Cook at **HIGH** 9 to
10½ minutes, or until chicken is tender.
Let stand, uncovered, 5 minutes before
serving.

*Note: For TWO Servings (4 pieces), follow
above procedure. Halve all
ingredients and cook chicken 5½ to
6 minutes.*
*For ONE Serving (2 pieces), cook
chicken 3½ to 4 minutes.*

114

HONEY GLAZED CHICKEN I-M

2 chicken breasts, split
¼ cup honey
2 tablespoons orange juice
1 tablespoon chili sauce
1 teaspoon prepared mustard
1 teaspoon browning sauce, optional

Yield: 4 Servings

Arrange chicken breasts in 12×8-inch dish with meatier portions toward edge of dish. Combine honey, orange juice, chili sauce, mustard and browning sauce; stir well. Pour honey mixture over chicken.

TO COOK BY INSTA-MATIC: Cover completely with plastic wrap. Cook on **COOK 4**. After time appears in display window; turn chicken pieces and rearrange.

TO COOK BY TIME: Cover with wax paper. Cook at **HIGH** 9 minutes and at **MEDIUM-LOW** 7 to 9 minutes. Halfway through cooking time turn chicken over and rearrange.

TO COMPLETE: Chicken should be tender. Let stand, uncovered, 5 minutes before serving.

HAWAIIAN ISLAND CHICKEN

2½ to 3 pound chicken, cut into serving pieces
2 tablespoons soy sauce
¼ teaspoon ginger
1 green pepper, cut into chunks
1 can (11 oz.) mandarin oranges, drained; reserve syrup
1 can (8¼ oz.) pineapple slices, drained and halved; reserve syrup
1 tablespoon cornstarch

Yield: 4 Servings

Arrange chicken in 12×8-inch dish with meatier portions toward edge of dish. Brush with soy sauce blended with ginger. Add green pepper. Cook, covered with wax paper, at **HIGH** 13 to 15 minutes; drain. Let stand, covered, 5 minutes.
In 2-cup glass measure, blend cornstarch with 1 cup reserved syrup until smooth. Cook at **HIGH** 2 minutes, stir once. Add fruit and pour over chicken. If necessary, reheat at **HIGH** 3 to 4 minutes.

CHICKEN IN WINE SAUCE

1 medium onion, sliced
¼ cup butter or margarine
2 boneless chicken breasts, skinned and thinly sliced (about 1 lb.)
Salt and pepper to taste
1 medium green pepper, cut into thin strips
⅓ cup white wine
1 jar (4½ oz.) sliced mushrooms, drained
2 tablespoons flour
⅔ cup chicken broth

Yield: 4 Servings

Combine onion and butter in 12×8-inch dish. Cook at **HIGH** 3 to 3½ minutes, or until onion is tender. Add chicken. Cook at **HIGH** 3 to 3½ minutes; stir once. Season with salt and pepper. Add green pepper and wine. Cook, covered with plastic wrap, at **HIGH** 2½ to 3 minutes. Add mushrooms. Blend flour with broth until smooth. Stir into dish. Cook at **HIGH** 3 to 4 minutes, or until sauce is thickened; stir twice.

115

CHICKEN PARMESAN

2 boneless chicken breasts, skinned, split and pounded thin (about 1 to 1¼ lb.)
¾ cup seasoned dry bread crumbs
¼ cup grated Parmesan cheese
¼ teaspoon paprika
1 egg, beaten with ¼ cup water
2 tablespoons oil
1 can (8 oz.) tomato sauce or 1 cup spaghetti sauce
Oregano
1 cup (4 oz.) shredded mozzarella cheese

Yield: 4 Servings

Dip chicken in bread crumbs mixed with Parmesan cheese and paprika, then in egg and again in bread crumb mixture. Coat bottom of 12×8-inch baking dish with 1 tablespoon oil. Place chicken in dish. Sprinkle with remaining oil. Cook at **HIGH** 2 to 2½ minutes. Turn chicken over and cook an additional 2 to 2½ minutes. Top with tomato sauce and season with oregano. Cook at **HIGH** 3½ to 4½ minutes, or until sauce is hot.
Sprinkle with mozzarella cheese and let stand, covered, 5 minutes or until cheese is melted.

Note: *For TWO Servings, follow above procedure; halve all ingredients. Cook chicken 1 to 1½ minutes each side and with tomato sauce 2 to 2½ minutes.*

BAKED CHICKEN WITH CORN BREAD STUFFING

1¼ to 1½ cups hot water
½ cup butter or margarine
1 package (6 oz.) corn bread stuffing mix with seasoning packet
3 chicken breasts, split (about 2½ lb.)
1 tablespoon butter or margarine, melted
¼ teaspoon browning sauce
1 can (10½ oz.) chicken gravy

Yield: 6 Servings

In 13×9-inch dish, combine water, ½ cup butter and seasoning packet. Cook at **HIGH** 3½ to 4 minutes. Stir in stuffing crumbs. Arrange chicken on stuffing with meatier portions toward edge of dish. Brush with melted butter mixed with browning sauce. Cook, covered with wax paper, at **HIGH** 12 to 13 minutes, or until chicken is tender. Let stand, covered, 5 minutes. Meanwhile, in small glass bowl, cook gravy at **HIGH** 3 to 3½ minutes stirring once. Serve over chicken.

ORIENTAL CHICKEN AND CASHEWS

3 tablespoons oil
2 boneless chicken breasts, skinned and thinly sliced (about 1 to 1¼ lb.)
2 cloves garlic, finely chopped
2 tablespoons soy sauce
1 tablespoon sherry
1 tablespoon cornstarch
¼ teaspoon ginger
1 medium green pepper, cut into small chunks
½ cup cashew halves or chopped walnuts

Yield: 4 Servings

Heat oil in 12×8-inch dish at **HIGH** 2½ to 3 minutes. Meanwhile, combine chicken, garlic, soy sauce, sherry, cornstarch and ginger. Add to dish and cook at **HIGH** 3 to 4 minutes; stir twice. Add green pepper and cashews. Cook, covered with plastic wrap, at **HIGH** 2½ to 3½ minutes, or until chicken and green pepper are tender; stir once. Let stand, 3 minutes before serving.

CHICKEN WITH SNOW PEAS

6 chicken legs, thighs detached (about 2¾ lb.)
1 tablespoon butter or margarine, melted
1 tablespoon soy sauce
1½ teaspoons paprika
½ teaspoon crushed rosemary
¼ teaspoon salt
1 package (6 oz.) frozen pea pods, defrost (see page 35)
1 jar (2½ oz.) sliced mushrooms, drained

Yield: 6 Servings

Arrange chicken in 12×8-inch dish. Combine butter, soy sauce, paprika, rosemary and salt. Brush over chicken. Cook, covered with wax paper, at **HIGH** 8 to 9 minutes. Top with pea pods and mushrooms. Cook, covered, at **HIGH** 5 to 6 minutes, or until chicken and vegetables are tender. Let stand, covered, 5 minutes before serving.

CHICKEN TERIYAKI I-M

2½ to 3 pound chicken, cut into serving pieces
1 can (8 oz.) chunk pineapple in pineapple juice
1 clove garlic, finely chopped
¼ cup soy sauce
2 tablespoons packed brown sugar
½ teaspoon salt
¼ teaspoon ginger

Yield: 4–6 Servings

Arrange chicken in 12×8-inch dish with meatier portions toward edge of dish. Combine remaining ingredients; stir well. Pour sauce over chicken.

TO COOK BY INSTA-MATIC: Cover completely with plastic wrap. Cook on **COOK 4.** After cooking, release plastic wrap.

TO COOK BY TIME: Cover with wax paper. Cook at **HIGH** 10 minutes and at **MEDIUM-LOW** 8 to 10 minutes.

TO COMPLETE: Chicken should be tender. Let stand, covered, 5 minutes. To serve, spoon pineapple sauce over chicken.

117

SPIRITED CHICKEN **I-M**

2½ pounds chicken legs, thighs detached
¼ cup dry sherry
2 tablespoons soy sauce
1½ teaspoons Worcestershire sauce
¼ teaspoon garlic salt

Yield: 5–6 Servings

Combine all ingredients in 12×8-inch dish. Marinate, if desired, 30 minutes.

TO COOK BY INSTA-MATIC: Cover completely with plastic wrap. Cook on **COOK 4.** After cooking, release plastic wrap.

TO COOK BY TIME: Cover with wax paper. Cook at **HIGH** 14 to 16 minutes, or until chicken is tender.

TO COMPLETE: Let stand, covered, 5 minutes before serving.

HERB BAKED CHICKEN **I-M**

1 teaspoon garlic salt
1 teaspoon paprika
½ teaspoon oregano
¼ teaspoon pepper
Juice and grated peel of 1 lemon
2½ to 3 pound chicken, cut into serving pieces
1 jar (4½ oz.) sliced mushrooms, drained

Yield: 4 Servings

Combine garlic, paprika, oregano, pepper and lemon peel. Rub over chicken. Arrange chicken in 12×8-inch dish with meatier portions toward edge of dish. Drizzle with lemon and top with mushrooms.

TO COOK BY INSTA-MATIC: Cover completely with plastic wrap. Cook on **COOK 4.** After cooking, release plastic wrap.

TO COOK BY TIME: Cover with wax paper. Cook at **HIGH** 10½ to 12 minutes.

TO COMPLETE: Chicken should be tender. Let stand, covered, 5 minutes before serving.

HURRY CURRY CHICKEN **I-M**

2½ to 3 pound chicken, cut into serving pieces
1 can (10¾ oz.) condensed cream of chicken soup
1 tomato, cut into wedges, optional
½ cup raisins or peanuts
1 tablespoon curry powder
1 tablespoon dried onion flakes
⅛ teaspoon garlic powder

Yield: 4 Servings

Arrange chicken, in 12×8-inch dish with meatier portions toward edge of dish. Combine remaining ingredients; mix well. Spoon over chicken.

TO COOK BY INSTA-MATIC: Cover completely with plastic wrap. Cook on **COOK 4.** After cooking, release plastic wrap.

TO COOK BY TIME: Cover with wax paper. Cook at **HIGH** 13 to 15 minutes.

TO COMPLETE: Chicken should be tender. Let stand, covered, 5 minutes. Remove chicken to serving platter. Stir sauce until smooth and serve over chicken.

TANGY CHICKEN CUTLETS

1 large onion, chopped
1 clove garlic, finely chopped
1 tablespoon water
4 chicken cutlets (1 lb.)
½ pound mushrooms, sliced
1 tablespoon tarragon or white wine vinegar
2 tablespoons flour
¼ cup water
½ teaspoon salt
⅛ teaspoon pepper
1 cup plain yogurt

Yield: 4 Servings

Combine onion, garlic, and water in 12×8-inch dish. Cover with plastic wrap. Cook at **HIGH** 4 to 5 minutes; stir once. Place cutlets in dish. Top with mushrooms and sprinkle with vinegar. Cover. Cook at **HIGH** 6½ to 7 minutes, or until chicken is tender. Halfway through cooking, rotate dish ½ turn.

Place chicken and vegetables on serving platter. Skim fat from liquid. Pour ¼ cup liquid into 1-quart glass bowl. Blend flour with ¼ cup water until smooth. Stir into liquid. Stir in salt, pepper and yogurt. Cook at **MEDIUM** 5 to 6 minutes or until thickened. Stir frequently. Pour sauce over cutlets and serve immediately.

STUFFED CORNISH HENS WITH ORANGE SAUCE

2½ cups hot water
1 can (6 oz.) frozen orange juice concentrate, defrosted and divided (see page 35)
1 package (6 oz.) long grain and wild rice mix
4 slices bacon, cooked and crumbled (see page 87)
4 cornish hens (1 lb. ea.)
⅓ cup honey
¼ to ½ teaspoon browning sauce

Yield: 4 Servings

In 2-quart casserole, combine water, ¼ cup orange juice concentrate and rice. Cook, covered with lid, at **HIGH** 5 to 6 minutes and at **MEDIUM-LOW** 20 minutes, or until rice is tender; stir in bacon. Stuff hens with rice mixture. With cotton string, tie legs together. Place hens in 12×8-inch dish. Cook, covered with wax paper, at **HIGH** 28 to 30 minutes, or until hens are tender.
Meanwhile, combine remaining orange juice concentrate, honey and browning sauce; brush hens every 10 minutes. Let stand covered, 10 minutes before serving.

CORNISH HENS WITH PEACH **I-M** SAUCE

2 cornish hens (about 1 lb. ea.) split
Browning sauce
Paprika
Pepper
1 can (16 oz.) sliced peaches in heavy syrup, drained; reserve ⅓ cup syrup
⅔ cup orange juice
1 tablespoon cornstarch
⅛ teaspoon ginger
Slivered almonds, optional

Yield: 4 Servings

Arrange hens in 12×8-inch dish, so that wings are in center of dish. Brush with browning sauce and season with paprika and pepper.

TO COOK BY INSTA-MATIC: Cover completely with 2 pieces of plastic wrap. Cook on **COOK 4**. After cooking, release plastic wrap.

TO COOK BY TIME: Cover with wax paper. Cook at **HIGH** 10 to 11 minutes.

TO COMPLETE: Hens should be tender. Let stand, covered, 7 minutes.
Meanwhile, in small glass bowl, combine reserved syrup, orange juice, cornstarch and ginger. Cook 1½ to 2½ minutes or until sauce is thickened; stir once. Add peaches and spoon over hens. If necessary, reheat 1½ to 2 minutes before serving. Garnish, if desired, with slivered almond.

*Note: **For TWO servings,** follow above procedure. Halve all ingredients. Cook hens 7 to 8 minutes. Add enough reserved syrup to orange juice to equal ½ cup. Cook sauce 1 to 1½ minutes.*

119

TURKEY DIVAN

2 packages (10 oz. ea.) frozen broccoli
  spears, defrosted (see page 35)
2 to 3 cups cut-up cooked turkey or
  chicken*
Salt and pepper to taste
1 can (11 oz.) condensed Cheddar cheese
  soup
½ cup milk
¼ cup buttered bread crumbs
½ teaspoon paprika

Yield: 4 Servings

Arrange broccoli in 12×8-inch dish; top
with turkey. Cook, covered with plastic
wrap, at **MEDIUM-HIGH** 5 to 6 minutes;
drain. Season with salt and pepper. In
small glass bowl, combine soup and milk.
Cook at **MEDIUM-HIGH** 2 to 3 minutes; stir
until smooth. Pour sauce over turkey.
Cook, covered, at **MEDIUM-HIGH** 5 to 6
minutes or until heated through.
Top with bread crumbs mixed with
paprika. Let stand, covered, 5 minutes
before serving.

If desired, turkey may be thinly sliced.

ROAST DUCK WITH ORANGE

4 to 5 pound duck
¼ cup bottled fruit sauce (for poultry)
2 tablespoons orange liqueur or orange
  juice
¼ teaspoon browning sauce
1 can (11 oz.) mandarin oranges, drained,
  optional

Yield: 4–6 Servings

Pierce skin of duck several times. Place
duck breast-side up on microwave roasting
rack set in 12×8-inch dish. Combine fruit
sauce, orange liqueur and browning sauce;
set aside. Cook at **MEDIUM** 30 minutes;
drain. Brush half of sauce on duck. Cook at
MEDIUM 20 to 25 minutes, or until duck is
tender.
Brush with remaining sauce. Let stand,
covered, 10 minutes before serving.
Garnish with orange.

PECAN STUFFED PHEASANT

½ cup thinly sliced celery
2 tablespoons butter or margarine
⅔ cup dry bread crumbs
⅓ cup chopped pecans
1 teaspoon salt, divided
⅛ teaspoon pepper
2 pheasants (1 to 1½ lb. ea.)
1 cup water, divided
2 to 3 tablespoons sherry
1 teaspoon browning sauce
2 tablespoons cornstarch

Yield: 4 Servings

Combine celery and butter in small glass
bowl. Cook at **HIGH** 1 to 2 minutes. Stir in
bread crumbs, pecans, ½ teaspoon salt
and pepper. Stuff pheasant with pecan
mixture. With cotton string, tie wings and
legs to body of pheasant. Arrange
pheasant breast-side up, in 8-inch square
dish. Add ¾ cup water, sherry and
browning sauce. Cook, covered with plastic
wrap, at **HIGH** 8 to 10 minutes and at
MEDIUM-LOW 18 to 20 minutes, or until
pheasant is tender. Remove pheasant to
serving platter. Let stand, covered, 5
minutes.
Blend cornstarch with remaining ¼ cup
water until smooth. Stir cornstarch and
salt into dish. Cook at **HIGH** 2 to 3
minutes, or until thickened, stir once.
Serve with pheasant.

ROAST WHOLE TURKEY

12 pound turkey
Salt
Poultry seasoning
Browning sauce

Yield: 12 Servings

Season inside of turkey with salt and poultry seasoning. Tuck wing tips beneath body and tie wings and legs together with cotton string. Arrange turkey breast-side down on microwave roasting rack set in 12×8-inch dish. Brush with browning sauce.

TO COOK BY TEMPERATURE: Cook at **MEDIUM** 4 minutes per pound.
Turn turkey breast-side up. Insert probe parallel to the leg, into the thickest portion of the thigh. The probe should be between the inner thigh and body of the bird and should not touch bones. Cook on Insta-Matic **TEMP 7** or Programmable Temp at **MEDIUM**, 140°F and at **MEDIUM-LOW**, 190°F. Drain liquid occasionally.

TO COOK BY TIME: Cook, covered with wax paper at **MEDIUM** for 48 minutes, draining liquid once. Turn turkey breast-side up; brush with browning sauce. Cook, covered with wax paper, at **MEDIUM-LOW** for 1¼ hours or until turkey registers 190°F when tested with conventional meat thermometer inserted in thigh joint as described below. (Remove roast from oven before reading temperature.)

TO COMPLETE: Let stand, covered, 20 minutes before serving.

Note: Turkey may be stuffed before heating. Close cavity with cotton string or wooden toothpicks. If necessary, halfway through cooking time or when turkey reaches 100°F, shield legs, wings and breast bone with aluminum foil to prevent overcooking.

ROAST GOOSE WITH APPLE STUFFING

¼ cup butter, margarine or goose fat
2 stalks celery, thinly sliced
2 medium onions, finely chopped
3 to 5 cups fresh bread cubes
2 medium apples, chopped
1 egg, beaten
¼ cup brandy
1 tablespoon parsley flakes
1 teaspoon salt
¼ teaspoon pepper
9 to 10 pound goose
Browning sauce

Yield: 6–8 Servings

In large glass bowl, combine butter, celery and onion. Cook at **HIGH** 5 to 6 minutes, or until celery and onion are tender. Add bread, apples, egg, brandy, parsley, salt and pepper; combine thoroughly. Stuff goose with apple mixture. Secure opening with wooden toothpicks or cotton string. Secure wings and legs to body of bird with cotton string. Pierce skin several times. Arrange bird breast-side down, on microwave roasting rack set in 12×8-inch dish. Brush with browning sauce. Cook at **MEDIUM** 30 minutes. Turn bird over and drain fat. Cook at **MEDIUM** 25 to 30 minutes, or until tender. Let stand, covered, 15 minutes before serving.

TURKEY ROAST

2 pound frozen turkey roast

Yield: 6 Servings

In glass loaf dish, place turkey roast gravy-side up; cover with plastic wrap. Heat at **MEDIUM-LOW** 17 minutes. Turn roast over; recover. Heat at **MEDIUM-LOW** 17 to 20 minutes, or until roast registers 160°F when tested with a conventional meat thermometer. (Remove roast from oven before reading temperature). Let stand, covered, 7 minutes before serving.

APPLE SAUSAGE STUFFING

½ pound bulk pork sausage
1 cup thinly sliced celery
1 large onion, finely chopped
5 cups fresh bread cubes
3 cups chopped apple (3 medium)
2 eggs, beaten
1 to 1½ teaspoons salt
¼ to ½ teaspoon poultry seasoning

Yield: 8 Servings (about 6 cups)

Crumble sausage in 12×8-inch dish. Stir in celery and onion. Cook at **HIGH** 4½ to 5½ minutes, or until sausage is browned, stir twice. Drain. Add remaining ingredients; combine thoroughly.* Cook, covered with plastic wrap, at **HIGH** 3 to 4 minutes and at **MEDIUM-LOW** 5 to 6 minutes, or until heated through.

*This makes enough to stuff a 7 to 9 lb. bird.

CORN BREAD STUFFING

1½ cups thinly sliced celery
1 large onion, chopped
½ cup butter or margarine
2 packages (12 oz. ea.) corn bread or corn muffin mix, baked and crumbled (see page 195)
2 eggs
1½ cups orange juice or chicken broth
1½ teaspoons salt
¾ teaspoon sage
¼ teaspoon pepper

Yield: 12 Servings (about 9 cups)

In 3-quart casserole, combine celery, onion and butter. Cook at **HIGH** 6 to 7 minutes, or until celery and onion are tender; stir twice. Add remaining ingredients; combine thoroughly.* Cook, covered with lid, at **MEDIUM-LOW** 10 to 11 minutes, or until heated through.
Let stand, covered, 5 minutes before serving.

*This makes enough to stuff a 9 to 12 pound bird.

CONVENIENCE STUFFING MIXES

1½ to 1¾ cups hot water
¼ cup butter
1 package (6 to 6½ oz.) stuffing mix (chicken, cornbread, pork or rice varieties) with seasoning packet

Yield: 6 Servings

In 2-quart casserole, combine water, butter and seasoning packet. Cook at **HIGH** 4½ to 5 minutes; stir in stuffing crumbs.*

Let stand, covered, 5 minutes before serving.

*This makes enough to stuff a 2½ to 3 pound bird.

Variations: Add one of the following with seasoning packet:
- 1 cup chopped fresh cranberries or apples
- ½ cup raisins, chopped nuts, or chopped apricots
- ½ pound browned ground sausage, drained
- 1 can (8 oz.) whole kernel corn, drained

FISH and SEAFOOD

Fish for dinner is always a delightful surprise to daily meal planning. And how lucky you seafood lovers are—fish prepared in the microwave oven is moist and delicious, not to mention quick.

Just follow the simple instructions in the charts or one of these tasty recipes and your efforts are sure to be applauded.

GENERAL DIRECTIONS FOR COOKING FISH AND SEAFOOD

Clean fish before starting the recipe. Arrange fish in a single layer; do not overlap edges. Place thicker pieces toward outside edge of dish. Shrimp and scallops should be placed in a single layer.

To Cook by Time: Cover dish with plastic wrap. Cook on the power level and for the minimum time recommended in chart on page 125. Halfway through cooking rearrange or stir shrimp or scallops.

To Cook by Insta-Matic: Cover dish completely with plastic wrap. Cook on Insta-Matic COOK setting listed in chart on page 125. When time appears in display window, stir shrimp or scallops.

Let stand, covered, 5 minutes.

Test for doneness before adding extra heating time. Fish and seafood should be opaque in color and fish should flake when tested with a fork. If undercooked, return to oven and continue to cook for 30 to 60 seconds.

COOKING FISH AND SEAFOOD ON INSTA-MATIC AND TIME I-M

FISH OR SEAFOOD	AMOUNT	POWER	APPROX. COOKING TIME (in minutes)	INSTA-MATIC SETTING
Fish Fillets	1 lb.	HIGH	4 to 6	———
Fish Steaks	4 (6 oz. ea.)	HIGH	6 to 8	———
Scallops (sea)	1 lb.	MEDIUM	6½ to 8½	COOK 7
Shrimp medium size (shelled and cleaned)	1 lb.	MEDIUM	4½ to 6½	COOK 7
Whole fish (stuffed or unstuffed)	1½ to 1¾ lb.	HIGH	9 to 11	COOK 4

Note: *Fish and seafood not listed above are not suitable for Insta-Matic cooking.*

125

FILLET PROVENCALE

2 small onions, sliced
2 tablespoons butter or margarine
1 clove garlic, finely chopped
1 can (16 oz.) stewed tomatoes, chopped
1 jar (4½ oz.) sliced mushrooms, drained
¼ cup white wine
⅛ teaspoon basil
6 flounder fillets (about ¼ lb. ea.)
Salt

Yield: 6 Servings

In 12×8-inch dish, combine onion, butter and garlic. Cook, covered with plastic wrap, at **HIGH** 3 to 3½ minutes. Stir in tomatoes, mushrooms, wine and basil. Cook, covered, at **HIGH** 3 minutes and at **MEDIUM** 3 to 4 minutes. Meanwhile, season fish with salt, skin side only. Roll up (skin-side in) and arrange seam-side down in sauce; spoon sauce over fish. Cook, covered, at **HIGH** 5 to 6 minutes, or until fish is done. Let stand, covered, 5 minutes before serving.

TROUT AMANDINE I-M

⅓ cup butter or margarine
½ cup slivered almonds
2 whole trout (about 12 oz. ea.) cleaned
Salt and pepper to taste
Lemon juice

Yield: 2–4 Servings

Combine butter and almonds in 2-cup glass measure. Cook at **HIGH** 3 to 4 minutes, or until almonds are lightly browned; stir twice.
Arrange fish in 12×8-inch dish. Season inside of fish with salt, pepper and lemon juice. Pour butter and almonds inside and over fish.

TO COOK BY INSTA-MATIC: Cover completely with plastic wrap. Cook on **COOK 4**. After cooking, release plastic wrap.

TO COOK BY TIME: Cover with wax paper. Cook at **HIGH** 6 to 7 minutes.

TO COMPLETE: Fish should be tender. Let stand, covered, 5 minutes before serving.

SCROD WITH GRAPE SAUCE

2 tablespoons butter or margarine
1 tablespoon dried onion flakes
¾ cup chicken broth
Pepper to taste
1½ pounds scrod or sole fillets
3 tablespoons flour
¾ cup milk or half'n half
1 cup halved green grapes
Parsley

Yield: 4–6 Servings

In 12×8-inch dish, combine butter, onion, broth and pepper. Cook at **HIGH** 2 to 3 minutes. Arrange fillets in single layer. Cook, covered with wax paper, at **HIGH** 7 to 8 minutes, or until fish is done. Arrange fillets on serving platter; cover. Strain broth into small glass bowl. Blend flour with milk until smooth. Stir milk and grapes into broth.
Cook at **MEDIUM** 3½ to 5 minutes, or until sauce is thickened; stir twice.
Pour half of sauce over fillets, sprinkle with parsley. Serve remaining sauce with fillets.

Variation: Add 2 tablespoons white wine when cooking fish.

PARCHMENT SEAFOOD SPECTACULAR I-M

2 tablespoons brandy
1 tablespoon lemon juice
4 halibut or other fish steaks (about 6 oz. ea.)
2 tablespoons butter or margarine
2 teaspoons dried chives
Salt and pepper to taste
1 cup sliced fresh mushrooms (about ¼ lb.)
1 small apple, thinly sliced

Yield: 4 Servings

In small bowl, combine brandy and lemon juice.

TO COOK BY INSTA-MATIC: Arrange fish in 12×8-inch dish; do NOT use parchment paper. Brush brandy mixture over fish; dot with ½ tablespoon butter, 1 teaspoon chives and season with salt and peper. Mound mushrooms and apples on top. Cover completely with plastic wrap. Cook on **COOK 7**. After cooking, release plastic wrap.

TO COOK BY TIME: Place each fish steak on a 10×5-inch piece of parchment paper. Brush fish with brandy mixture. Dot with 2 tablespoons butter. Season with chives, salt and pepper. Mound mushrooms and apples on top; bring paper up around fish. Fold edges over twice to seal top; fold side edges up. Place on glass oven tray. Cook at **HIGH** 7½ to 9 minutes.

TO COMPLETE: Let stand 5 minutes before serving packet directly on dinner plate.

FLOUNDER WITH SHRIMP SAUCE I-M

4 flounder fillets (about ¼ lb. ea.)
1 can (10¾ oz.) condensed cream of shrimp soup
¼ cup white wine or milk
½ cup (2 oz.) shredded Swiss cheese
Parsley or slivered almonds

Yield: 4 Servings

Roll up fillets and arrange seam-side down in 8-inch square dish. Combine soup, wine and cheese; spoon over fillets.

TO COOK BY INSTA-MATIC: Cover completely with plastic wrap. Cook on **COOK 7**. After cooking, release plastic wrap.

TO COOK BY TIME: Cover with plastic wrap. Cook at **MEDIUM** 11 to 12 minutes, or until fish is done.

TO COMPLETE: Let stand, covered, 5 minutes. Sprinkle with parsley or almonds before serving.

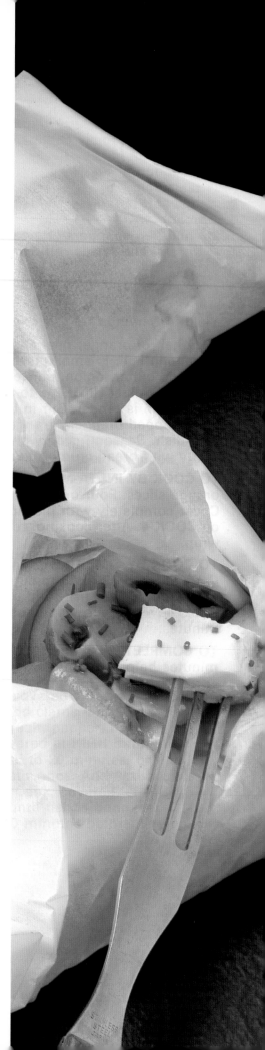

SHEPHERD'S PIE

1 large onion, chopped
3 tablespoons butter or margarine
½ tablespoon parsley flakes
1½ cups beef gravy
2 cups cut-up cooked lamb or beef
  (about ¾-inch pieces)
1 package (10 oz.) frozen peas and carrots,
  defrosted (see page 35)
1½ to 2 cups hot mashed potatoes
Paprika

Yield: 4 Servings

Combine onion and butter in 2-quart casserole. Cook at **HIGH** 2 to 2½ minutes, or until onion is tender. Stir in parsley; gradually add gravy. Cook at **HIGH** 3 to 4 minutes, or until gravy is hot; stir twice. Stir in lamb and peas and carrots. Cook at **MEDIUM-HIGH** 10 to 11 minutes, or until heated through; stir twice. Spoon potatoes on top of casserole; sprinkle with paprika. Cook at **MEDIUM-HIGH** 2 to 3 minutes.

CORN DOGGIES

¼ cup butter or margarine
1 medium onion, chopped
1 can (8 oz.) cream-style corn
½ cup milk
1 egg, beaten
⅛ teaspoon hot pepper sauce
¾ cup yellow cornmeal
¾ cup flour
1 tablespoon sugar
2 teaspoons baking powder
½ teaspoon salt
¼ teaspoon dry mustard
4 to 5 frankfurters, cut crosswise in thirds

Yield: 4 Servings

Combine butter and onion in glass bowl. Cook at **HIGH** 2½ minutes; stir once. Stir in corn, milk, egg and hot pepper sauce until smooth. Add cornmeal, flour, sugar, baking powder, salt and mustard. Place frankfurter pieces in spoke fashion in greased 2-quart ring mold. Pour cornmeal mixture over frankfurters. Cook at **MEDIUM-LOW** 13 to 16 minutes, or until toothpick comes out clean. Let stand 5 minutes before serving.

QUICK CORNED BEEF AND CABBAGE

2 medium potatoes, thinly sliced (about 2
  cups)
1 medium onion, sliced
¼ cup water
¾ teaspoon salt
⅛ teaspoon pepper
1 can (12 oz.) corned beef, crumbled
½ head cabbage, cut into 4 wedges (about
  1¼ lb.)
¼ cup butter or margarine, melted*

Yield: 4 Servings

In greased 3-quart casserole, layer potatoes and onion. Add water, salt and pepper. Cook, covered with lid, at **HIGH** 8 to 9 minutes. Add corned beef and cabbage; pour butter over cabbage. Heat, covered, at **HIGH** 10 to 12 minutes, or until cabbage is tender. Let stand, covered, 5 minutes before serving.

HOT ENCHILADA DOGS I-M

1 can (16 oz.) chili without beans
3 tablespoons finely chopped green chili
  peppers
⅛ teaspoon hot pepper sauce
8 tortillas, softened*
8 frankfurters, ends slit
1 can (8 oz.) tomato sauce
1 cup (4 oz.) shredded Cheddar cheese

Yield: 4 Servings

Combine chili, chili peppers and hot pepper
sauce. Place 2 tablespoons chili mixture on
each tortilla; place frankfurters in center
and roll up. Arrange tortillas seam-side
down in 12×8-inch dish. Combine tomato
sauce with remaining chili mixture; pour
over tortillas. Cover completely with plastic
wrap.

TO COOK BY INSTA-MATIC: Cook on
COOK 8.

TO COOK BY TIME: Cook at **MEDIUM-HIGH**
6½ to 7½ minutes.

TO COMPLETE: Top with cheese. Let stand,
covered, 5 minutes before serving.

Hint: To soften tortillas in your
microwave oven, place tortillas on paper
plates. Cover with wax paper. Heat at
HIGH 40 to 60 seconds or until softened.

PARTY TUNA CASSEROLE

2 tablespoons butter or margarine, melted
1 tablespoon soy sauce
1 can (3 oz.) chow mein noodles
1 can (10¾ oz.) condensed cream of
  mushroom soup
1 can (7 oz.) tuna, drained and flaked
1 cup finely chopped celery
¼ pound salted cashew nuts
2 teaspoons dried onion flakes
¼ cup water

Yield: 4 Servings

Combine butter, soy sauce, and noodles;
toss well and reserve. In 8-inch round dish,
combine soup, tuna, celery, nuts, onion
and water. Cook at **MEDIUM-HIGH** 9 to 10
minutes, or until heated through; stir
twice. Top with noodles and heat at
MEDIUM-HIGH 1 minute. Let stand,
covered, 5 minutes.

COUNTRY HAM CASSEROLE

1 can (10¾ oz.) condensed cream of celery
  soup
¾ cup milk
½ teaspoon dry mustard, optional
1 package (8 oz.) noodles, cooked
  (see pages 184 and 185)
2 cups cut-up cooked ham (about ¾ lb.)
1½ cups (6 oz.) shredded Swiss cheese,
  divided
1 can (16 oz.) green peas, drained
French fried onion pieces or crushed
  corn chips

Yield: 4 Servings

In 3-quart casserole, combine soup, milk
and mustard. Stir in noodles, ham, 1¼
cups cheese and peas; cover with plastic
wrap. Cook at **MEDIUM-HIGH** 12 to 14
minutes. Stir twice. Top with remaining
cheese and onion pieces. Let stand,
covered, 5 minutes before serving.

MERMAID'S IMPERIAL DELIGHT

¼ cup chopped green pepper
2 tablespoons butter or margarine
1 pound medium shrimp, shelled and
  cleaned
2 cup cooked rice (see pages 187 and 188)
¾ cups mayonnaise
1 can (8 oz.) peas, drained
1 package (6 oz.) crabmeat, drained and
  flaked (canned or frozen, defrosted see
  page 33)
Salt and pepper to taste

Yield: 6 Servings

In 2-quart casserole, combine green pepper
and butter. Cook at **HIGH** 1½ minutes; stir
once. Add shrimp and cook at **MEDIUM** 2
minutes; stir once. Stir in remaining
ingredients. Cook, covered with lid, at
MEDIUM 8 to 9 minutes, or until heated
through, stir twice.
Top, if desired, with buttered bread
crumbs.

PAELLA

5½ cups hot tap water
½ teaspoon cinnamon
Pinch saffron
2 packages (6 oz. ea.) chicken flavored rice mix with flavor packet
6 pieces frozen fried chicken, defrosted (see page 38)
1 package (9 oz.) frozen artichoke hearts, defrosted (see page 35)
½ cup sliced pitted ripe olives, optional
3 tablespoons chopped pimento, optional
12 small clams, scrubbed
12 medium shrimp, shelled and cleaned
¾ pound cooked ham, cubed

Yield: 6 Servings

In 5-quart casserole, combine water, cinnamon, saffron and flavor packets from rice mix. Cook, covered with lid, at **HIGH** 10 to 12 minutes, or until liquid is boiling. Add rice; cook, covered, at **HIGH** 10 to 11 minutes. Add chicken, artichokes, olives and pimento. Cook, covered, at **MEDIUM** 10 to 11 minutes, stir once. Add clams and let stand, covered, 10 to 12 minutes. Add shrimp and ham and cook, covered, at **MEDIUM** 11 to 12 minutes, stir once. Let stand 10 minutes.

SPICY SHRIMP AND SPAGHETTI BAKE

½ cup chopped green pepper
1 medium onion, chopped
3 tablespoons butter or margarine
2 cans (8 oz. ea.) tomato sauce
1 can (16 oz.) whole tomatoes, chopped
1 tablespoon Worcestershire sauce
1 teaspoon salt
⅛ teaspoon crushed red pepper, optional
1 pound medium shrimp, shelled and cleaned
1 package (8 oz.) spaghetti, cooked and drained (see pages 184 and 185)
¾ cup grated Parmesan cheese, divided

Yield: 4–6 Servings

In 3-quart casserole, combine green pepper, onion and butter. Cook, covered with lid, at **HIGH** 3 to 4 minutes. Stir in tomato sauce, tomatoes, Worcestershire sauce, salt and red pepper. Cook, covered, at **HIGH** 8 to 9 minutes, stir once. Stir in spaghetti and shrimp. Cook, covered, at **MEDIUM** 9 to 11 minutes, or until shrimp are done and mixture is hot; stir twice. Stir in ½ cup cheese. Top with remaining cheese. Let stand 5 minutes.

NONA'S ITALIAN SAUSAGE

1½ pounds Italian sausage links, cut into
    1½-inch pieces
3 medium potatoes, peeled and cut into
    small chunks
1 clove garlic, finely chopped
3 medium green peppers, cut into chunks
3 medium onions, cut into chunks
2 cans (8 oz. ea.) tomato sauce
½ teaspoon salt
½ teaspoon oregano
¼ teaspoon pepper

Yield: 6 Servings

In 3-quart casserole, combine sausage,
potatoes and garlic. Cook, covered with lid,
at **HIGH** 11 to 13 minutes, or until potatoes
are tender; stir twice. Drain; stir in
remaining ingredients and cook, covered,
at **HIGH** 12 to 13* minutes, or until
vegetables are tender; stir twice.
Let stand, covered, 5 minutes before
serving.

*If desired, add an additional can (8 oz.)
  tomato sauce.

HONEYED HAM AND APPLE RING

1¼ pounds cooked ham, ground
    (about 3½ cups)
5 small apples, divided
3 eggs
1 cup soft bread crumbs
½ cup milk
⅓ cup finely chopped onion
5 tablespoons honey, divided
¼ teaspoon cloves
⅛ teaspoon ginger
Pepper to taste
2 tablespoons butter or margarine

Yield: 6 Servings

Combine ham, 1 apple chopped, eggs,
bread crumbs, milk, onion, 4 tablespoons
honey, cloves, ginger and pepper. Spoon
mixture into greased 2-quart ring mold.
Cover with wax paper. Cook at **MEDIUM-
HIGH** 13 to 15 minutes, or until mixture is
set. Let stand, covered, 7 minutes.
Meanwhile, peel and slice remaining
apples. In small glass bowl, combine
apples, butter and remaining honey. Cook,
covered with plastic wrap, at **HIGH** 6 to 7
minutes, or until apples are tender. Stir
once. Invert ham onto serving platter;
arrange apples on top of ring.

SAUSAGE AND BEAN CASSOULET

1½ pounds Italian sausage links, cut into
    1½-inch pieces
2 small onions, sliced
2 cans (16 oz. ea.) navy or small white
    beans, rinsed*
½ pound cooked ham, cut into 1-inch
    pieces
1 can (8 oz.) tomato sauce
½ cup catsup
¼ cup white wine or water
¼ cup packed brown sugar
1 teaspoon salt
½ teaspoon dry mustard
½ teaspoon pepper

Yield: 6 Servings

Combine sausage and onions in 3-quart
casserole. Cook, covered with lid, at **HIGH**
8 to 10 minutes, or until sausage is almost
cooked; stir once. Drain. Stir in remaining
ingredients and cook, covered, at **HIGH** 5
minutes and at **MEDIUM** 10 to 15 minutes,
or until flavors are blended; stir twice.

*Note: To use dried beans, see page 174.

143

BAKED ZITI

1 package (8 oz.) ziti macaroni, cooked (see pages 184 and 185)
1 jar (15½ oz.) spaghetti sauce
½ cup (2 oz.) shredded mozzarella cheese

Yield: 4 Servings

In 2-quart casserole, combine ziti and spaghetti sauce. Cook, covered with lid, at **MEDIUM-HIGH** 8 to 9 minutes; stir once. Sprinkle with cheese. Let stand, covered, 10 minutes before serving.

EASY LASAGNA

½ pound ground beef
1 jar (15½ oz.) spaghetti sauce
1 can (8 oz.) tomato sauce
1 tablespoon oregano
½ teaspoon garlic powder
1½ cups ricotta or cottage cheese
½ cup grated Romano cheese
1 egg, lightly beaten
⅛ teaspoon pepper
9 lasagna noodles cooked and drained (see pages 184 and 185)
1 pkg. (8 oz.) shredded mozzarella cheese
½ cup grated Parmesan cheese

Yield: 6 Servings

Crumble ground beef in large bowl. Cook at **HIGH** 3 to 4 minutes, or until beef is browned; stir once. Drain. Stir in spaghetti sauce, tomato sauce, and seasonings. Meanwhile, combine ricotta cheese, Romano cheese, egg and pepper. Spoon ½ cup sauce in 12×8-inch dish; alternately layer noodles, egg mixture, mozzarella cheese and sauce, forming 3 layers. Cover completely with plastic wrap.

TO COOK BY INSTA-MATIC: Cook on **Cook 3**. If necessary, shield ends of dish with foil, during last 10 minutes of cooking.

TO COOK BY TIME: Cook at **HIGH** 8 minutes and at **MEDIUM-LOW** 32 to 34 minutes, or until noodles are tender. If necessary, shield ends of dish with foil, during last 10 minutes of cooking.

TO COMPLETE: Sprinkle with Parmesan cheese; let stand, covered, 15 minutes before serving.

EGGPLANT PARMESAN

1 large eggplant (about 1¾ lb.)
1 slice white bread, crumbled
¼ cup grated Parmesan cheese
2 tablespoons butter or margarine, melted
2 cups spaghetti sauce
1½ to 2 cups (6 to 8 oz.) shredded mozzarella cheese

Yield: 4 Servings

Pierce skin of eggplant several times. Place eggplant on paper towel on glass oven tray. Cook at **HIGH** 5 to 6 minutes, or until eggplant is almost tender; roll over twice. Let cool, then peel, if desired, and cut into ½-inch slices.
Meanwhile, combine bread, Parmesan cheese and butter. In 8-inch square dish, alternately layer spaghetti sauce, eggplant, crumb mixture and mozzarella cheese. Cover with wax paper. Cook at **HIGH** 14 to 16 minutes, or until hot and bubbly. Let stand, covered 5 minutes before serving.

EGGS and CHEESES

With the assistance of your microwave oven you can have poached eggs in minutes. Cook directly in the serving bowl. And, you won't be left with the dirty dishes. Creamy scrambled eggs, smooth Welsh rarebit, easy Omelets—all this and more awaits you in this chapter.

DIRECTIONS FOR BAKED EGGS

Generously grease 6-ounce custard cup for each egg. Break egg into cup and with toothpick, pierce egg yolk twice and egg white several times.

Top with one teaspoon milk.

Cover with plastic wrap and cook at MEDIUM according to time indicated in chart.

Let stand before serving. Serve over toast.

BAKED EGGS

NUMBER OF EGGS	APPROX. COOKING TIME (in minutes) at MEDIUM*	STAND TIME
1	¾ to 1	1
2	1¼ to 1½	1
4	1¾ to 2¼	1½
6	2½ to 3	2

*Note: *Eggs will be slightly underdone after cooking time. The cooking will be completed during stand time.*

DIRECTIONS FOR POACHED EGGS

Use 10-ounce custard cup or small glass bowl for each egg. In each cup heat at HIGH ¼ cup hot water and a dash of vinegar and salt.

Break egg into boiling water and with toothpick, pierce egg yolk twice and egg white several times.

Cover with plastic wrap. Cook at MEDIUM according to time indicated in chart.

Let stand, covered. Serve on buttered toast or your favorite way.

POACHED EGGS

NUMBER OF EGGS	APPROX. COOKING TIME (in minutes)		STAND TIME
	TO BOIL WATER at HIGH	TO POACH EGGS at MEDIUM*	
1	1	½ to ¾	1
2	3	1½ to 1¾	2
4	4	2¼ to 2½	2
6	6 to 6½	3½ to 3¾	2

*Note: *Eggs will be slightly underdone after cooking time. The cooking will be completed during standing time.*

DIRECTIONS FOR SCRAMBLED EGGS

Beat eggs. For each egg add 1 tablespoon milk and dash of salt. Pour into a greased glass container.

Cook at MEDIUM according to time in the chart. Between first and second cooking time, stir eggs. Bring cooked portions along edge of dish to center.

Stir and let stand.

Eggs will continue to cook during stand time and should be slightly underdone after cooking.

SCRAMBLED EGGS

NUMBER OF EGGS	CONTAINER	APPROX. COOKING TIME (in minutes) at MEDIUM*		STAND TIME
		FIRST COOKING	SECOND COOKING	
1	1 cup glass measure	½ to ¾	¼ to ½	1
2	1 cup glass measure	¾ to 1	½ to ¾	1½
4	1 qt. glass bowl	1¾ to 2½	1 to 1½	1½
6	1½ qt. glass bowl	2½ to 3	1 to 1½	2
8	1½ qt. glass bowl	3 to 3¼	2 to 2½	2

*Note: Eggs will be slightly underdone after cooking time. The cooking will be completed during stand time.

DIRECTIONS FOR HARD-COOKED EGGS

Eggs should not be hard-cooked in their shell in a microwave oven. Pressure will build up and the egg will explode. However, if the hard-cooked egg will be chopped or sieved, it may be cooked in the microwave oven. Grease 6-ounce custard cups for each egg. Break egg into cup and with toothpick, pierce egg yolk twice and egg white several times.

Cover with plastic wrap and cook at MEDIUM for the time recommended in the chart.

Let stand to cool before slicing, chopping, etc.

HARD-COOKED EGGS

NUMBER OF EGGS	APPROX. COOKING TIME (in minutes) at MEDIUM
1	1 to 1½
2	2 to 2½
4	3½ to 4

149

NORMANDY OMELET

1 small apple, sliced
2 tablespoons butter or margarine, divided
1 tablespoon honey
Dash cinnamon
4 eggs, separated
Salt and pepper to taste

Yield: 2 Servings

In small glass bowl, combine apple, 1 tablespoon butter, honey and cinnamon. Cook, covered with plastic wrap, at **HIGH** 2 to 3 minutes, or until apples are tender; reserve. Heat remaining butter in 9-inch pie plate at **MEDIUM-LOW** ½ to ¾ minute, or until melted; turn plate to coat bottom with butter.
Meanwhile, beat egg whites until stiff, but not dry; beat egg yolks, salt and pepper until thickened. Fold egg yolks into egg whites; carefully pour mixture into pie plate. Cook at **MEDIUM** 4 to 5 minutes. Let stand 2 minutes. With spatula, loosen edges of omelet from plate; spoon apples onto half. Fold other half omelet over apples. Sprinkle, if desired, with confectioners sugar.

BASIC OMELET

1 tablespoon butter or margarine
2 eggs
2 tablespoons milk
⅛ teaspoon salt
Dash pepper

Yield: 1 Serving

Heat butter in 9-inch pie plate at **HIGH** ½ to ¾ minute, or until melted, turn plate to coat bottom with butter.
Meanwhile, combine remaining ingredients; pour into pie plate. Cook, covered with plastic wrap, at **MEDIUM** 2 to 3 minutes, or until omelet is almost set; stir after 1 minute. Let stand, covered, 2 minutes. With spatula, loosen edges of omelet from plate; fold into thirds to serve.

Note: Try one of these easy variations:
For CHEESE Omelet, before folding, sprinkle ¼ cup shredded cheese down center of omelet.
For HAM Omelet, before folding, sprinkle ¼ cup finely chopped cooked ham down center of omelet.
For HERB Omelet, blend in ⅛ teaspoon basil, thyme or crushed rosemary with eggs and milk.
For JELLY Omelet, before folding, spoon ¼ cup jelly down center of omelet.

150

BAKED EGGS IN BOLOGNA CUPS

4 slices bologna
4 eggs
Salt and pepper to taste

Yield: 4 Servings

For each serving, line each custard cup (6 oz. ea.) with bologna. Break egg into center. With toothpick, pierce egg yolk twice and egg white several times. Season with salt and pepper. Cover each cup with plastic wrap. Cook at **MEDIUM** 2 to 3 minutes. Let stand, covered, 2 minutes before serving.

*NOTE: **For TWO baked eggs,** follow above procedure; halve all ingredients. Cook 1¼ to 1¾ minutes. Let stand 1 minute.*

RANCHERO EGGS

1 can (28 oz.) stewed tomatoes, chopped
3 tablespoons chopped green chilies
1 tablespoon dried onion flakes
⅛ teaspoon garlic powder
Salt and pepper to taste
6 eggs
¾ cup (3 oz.) shredded Monterey jack or Cheddar cheese

Yield: 6 Servings

In 12×8-inch dish, combine tomatoes, chilies, onion, garlic, salt and pepper. Cook, covered with plastic wrap, at **HIGH** 4½ to 5½ minutes; stir once. Break eggs into tomato mixture (around outside edge); with toothpick, pierce egg yolks twice and egg whites several times. Cook, covered, at **MEDIUM** 4½ to 5½ minutes, or until eggs are almost set. Sprinkle with cheese. Let stand, covered, 5 minutes. If desired, serve over corn bread.

EGGS BENEDICT

1 package (1¼ oz.) hollandaise sauce mix
Ingredients as sauce mix package directs
4 eggs
4 thin slices cooked ham
2 English muffins, split and toasted

Yield: 4 Servings

Combine sauce mix and ingredients as package directs in 2-cup glass measure. Cook at **HIGH** 2 to 2½ minutes or until sauce is thickened; stir once. Prepare Poached Eggs according to chart, page 147. While eggs are standing cook ham. Arrange ham in a single layer on a paper towel lined paper plate. Cook at **MEDIUM** 1 to 1½ minutes.
To serve, place ham on muffin; top with egg, then sauce. If necessary, reheat at **MEDIUM** ½ to 1 minute.

SATURDAY'S HAM AND EGG SCRAMBLE

1 cup cut-up cooked ham
2 tablespoons butter or margarine
1 package (3 oz.) cream cheese, softened (see page 234)
⅓ cup milk
5 eggs
Salt and pepper to taste

Yield: 4 Servings

Combine ham and butter in 8-inch round dish. Covered with wax paper. Cook at **HIGH** 2 to 3 minutes; stir once. Combine cream cheese and milk; blend in eggs, salt and pepper. Add to ham. Cook, covered, at **MEDIUM** 5 to 6 minutes, or until eggs are almost set; stir twice. Let stand, covered, 3 minutes before serving.

CORNED BEEF HASH AND EGGS

1 can (24 oz.) corned beef hash
2 tablespoons catsup
1 tablespoon Worcestershire sauce
½ teaspoon onion powder
⅛ teaspoon pepper
4 eggs

Yield: 4 Servings

In 8-inch round baking dish, combine hash, catsup, Worcestershire, onion powder and pepper. Cook, covered with plastic wrap, at **MEDIUM-HIGH** 3 to 4 minutes; stir. Lightly pat mixture into dish and form 4 wells. Into each well, break 1 egg; with toothpick, pierce egg yolk twice and egg white several times. Cook, covered, at **MEDIUM** 3½ to 4½ minutes, or until eggs are almost set.
Let stand, covered, 5 minutes before serving.

COUNTRY BREAKFAST

2 medium baking potatoes (about 6 oz. ea.)*
¼ cup butter or margarine
¼ cup chopped green pepper
¼ cup chopped onion
4 eggs
½ cup milk
½ teaspoon salt
⅛ teaspoon pepper
2 slices American cheese, halved, optional

Yield: 4 Servings

Cook potatoes according to directions for baking potatoes (pages 167 and 169). Let stand 5 minutes; peel and slice. Meanwhile, in 8-inch round dish, combine butter, green pepper and onion. Cook at **HIGH** 3 to 4 minutes, or until vegetables are tender; add sliced potatoes. Combine eggs, milk, salt and pepper; stir into potatoes. Cook, covered with plastic wrap, at **MEDIUM** 5 to 6 minutes, or until eggs are set; stir twice.
Top with cheese. Let stand, covered, 5 minutes before serving.

***Substitution:** Use 1 or 2 cans (16 oz. ea.) sliced potatoes, drained for baked potatoes.*

MACARONI AND CHEESE

1 package (8 oz.) elbow macaroni, cooked
  and drained (see pages 184 and 185)
¾ pound pasteurized process cheese
  spread, cut into cubes
¾ to 1 cup milk
½ to ¾ teaspoon salt
¼ teaspoon onion powder
⅛ teaspoon dry mustard, optional
¼ teaspoon pepper
Buttered bread crumbs

Yield: 4 Servings

In 3-quart casserole, combine macaroni,
cheese, milk, salt, onion, mustard and
pepper. Cook, covered with lid, at **MEDIUM**
9 to 10 minutes; stir twice. Top with bread
crumbs and cook, uncovered, at **MEDIUM** 3
minutes.

Variation: Use ½ cup tomato sauce for ¼
cup milk and ⅛ teaspoon oregano for dry
mustard.

SPINACH CHEESE RING I-M

2 packages (10 oz. ea.) frozen chopped
  spinach, cooked and drained
  (see pages 167 and 169)
1 cup (½ pt.) cottage cheese
2 eggs
1 tablespoon caraway seeds
Dash pepper
¼ cup buttered seasoned bread crumbs
1 tablespoon grated Parmesan cheese
¼ teaspoon paprika

Yield: 4 Servings

In bowl, combine spinach, cottage cheese,
eggs, caraway seeds and pepper. Spoon
into 1-quart glass ring mold. Cover with
plastic wrap.

TO COOK BY INSTA-MATIC: Cook on
COOK 7.

TO COOK BY TIME: Cook at **MEDIUM** 4 to
5 minutes, or until almost set.

TO COMPLETE: Combine bread crumbs,
cheese and paprika. Sprinkle on top. Cook,
uncovered, at **MEDIUM** 1 to 1½ minutes.
Let stand, uncovered, 5 minutes.

HAMBURGERS... YOUR WAY

1 pound ground beef
4 slices each cheese, onion and tomato
4 hamburger rolls
Catsup or creamy Russian dressing

Yield: 4 Servings

Shape ground beef into 4 patties (about 4-in. in diameter). In 8-inch square dish, arrange patties. Heat **MEDIUM-HIGH** 3½ to 4½ minutes; turn patties over and drain liquid once.
Top with cheese. Let stand, covered, 2 minutes. Place each hamburger in roll and top with remaining ingredients, as desired.

Note: *For TWO Servings, follow above procedure. Halve all ingredients. Cook patties 1½ to 2 minutes.*
For ONE Serving, cook patty ¾ to 1¼ minutes.

CHILI TACOS

1 pound ground beef
1 package (1¼ oz.) taco seasoning mix
½ cup water
12 taco shells
1 cup shredded lettuce
⅔ cup chopped tomatoes
¼ cup chopped green pepper or onion
1 cup (4 oz.) shredded Cheddar or Monterey jack cheese

Yield: 6 Servings

Cook ground beef in 2-quart casserole at **HIGH** 3 to 4 minutes, or until browned. Stir once; drain. Add seasoning mix and water; cover with lid. Cook at **HIGH** 2 minutes and at **MEDIUM** 5 minutes; stir once.
Stir; let stand, covered, 3 minutes. Fill taco shells with 2 tablespoons beef mixture, then top with lettuce, tomato, green pepper and cheese*.

***Hint:** If desired, arrange taco shells in 12×8-inch baking dish; fill as directed above. Cook at **MEDIUM** 3 to 4 minutes to melt cheese.*

MEAT LOAF MELTWICH

Chili sauce
8 slices rye bread
8 thin slices cooked meat loaf
4 slices (rectangular) muenster cheese, halved

Yield: 4 Servings

Spread chili sauce on bread. On four slices, place meat loaf and cheese; top with remaining bread. Wrap each sandwich in paper napkin; arrange on glass oven tray. Cook at **MEDIUM** 2½ to 3½ minutes, or until heated through.

Note: *For TWO sandwiches, follow above procedure; halve all ingredients. Cook 1½ to 2 minutes.*
For ONE sandwich, cook 1 to 1½ minutes.

158

SLOPPY JOES

1 pound ground beef
½ cup finely chopped onion
½ to ¾ cup catsup
¼ cup sweet pickled relish
Salt and pepper to taste
4 hamburger rolls

Yield: 4 Servings

Crumble ground beef in 2-quart casserole. Stir in onion. Cook at **HIGH** 3 to 4 minutes, or until beef is browned. Stir once; drain. Stir in catsup, relish, salt and pepper. Cover with lid. Cook at **HIGH** 1½ to 2½ minutes and at **MEDIUM** 3 to 4 minutes. Stir once. Serve in split hamburger rolls.

Variation: Add ½ pound frankfurters sliced with ground beef.

OPEN FACED SANDWICHES WITH GRAVY

1 envelope (⅞ oz.) turkey gravy mix*
1 cup water*
½ pound sliced cooked turkey
4 slices white bread

Yield: 4 Servings

Combine gravy mix and water in 2-cup glass measure. Cook at **HIGH** 2½ to 3 minutes, or until thickened; stir twice. Arrange turkey in four piles (to fit bread) in 8-inch square dish. Cook, covered with plastic wrap, at **MEDIUM-HIGH** 1½ to 2 minutes, or until heated through. Arrange turkey on bread; top with gravy.

***Substitution:** Use 1 can (10½ oz.) mushroom gravy or 1 cup leftover gravy for mix and water. Cook 1½ to 2 minutes, stirring once.*

Note: *Chicken, pork or beef gravy and meat may be used.*

SEAFARER'S SANDWICH

1 package (8 oz.) frozen fried fish fillets (4 fillets)
½ cup cole slaw, optional
4 slices American cheese
4 hamburger rolls
4 tablespoons tartar sauce or cocktail sauce

Yield: 4 Servings

Cook fillets in 8-inch square dish at **MEDIUM-HIGH** 3½ to 4½ minutes. Top with cole slaw and cheese. Cook at **MEDIUM** 2½ to 3½ minutes, or until cheese is melted. Place fillet in roll; top with tartar sauce.

Note: *For TWO Servings, follow above procedure; halve all ingredients. Cook fillets 1½ to 2 minutes and cheese 1¼ to 1¾ minutes.*
For ONE Serving, cook fillet ¾ to 1¼ minutes and cheese ½ to 1 minute.

159

VEGETABLES	AMOUNT	APPROX. COOKING TIME, covered, at HIGH (in minutes)	STAND TIME (in minutes)
ARTICHOKES Fresh, about 6 to 8 oz. ea. (3-in. diameter) See recipe, page 176	1 2 4	6 to 7½ 8½ to 10 12½ to 14	5 5 5
Frozen, hearts	1 package (9 oz.) plus 1 T. water	5 to 6	3
ASPARAGUS Fresh, cut into 1½-in. pieces	1 pound plus 2T. water	5 to 6½	3
Frozen, spears	1 package (10 oz.) plus 1 T. water	5½ to 7	3
BEANS, Green or Wax Fresh, cut into 1½-in. pieces	1 pound plus 2 T. water	6½ to 8	3
Frozen	1 package (9 oz.) plus 1 T. water	6 to 8	3
BEETS Fresh, sliced	1½ to 2 pounds plus 2 T. water	10½ to 12	5
BROCCOLI Fresh, cut into spears	1 pound plus 2 T. water	6 to 7½	3
Frozen, chopped or spears	1 package (10 oz.) plus 1 T. water	6½ to 8	3
BRUSSEL SPROUTS Fresh	1 tub (10 oz.) plus 1 T. water 1 pound plus 2 T. water	8 to 10	5 5
Frozen	1 package (10 oz.) plus 1 T. water	7½ to 9	
CABBAGE, Fresh Chopped or Shredded	4 cups (about 1 lb.) plus 2 T. water	6½ to 8	5
Wedges	4 (about 1 lb.) plus 2 T. water	6 to 7½	5
CARROTS, sliced ½-in thick Fresh	1 pound plus 2 T. water	7 to 8½	5
Frozen	1 package (10 oz.) plus 1 T. water	5½ to 7	3
CAULIFLOWER Fresh, cut into flowerets	1 pound plus 2 T. water	6½ to 8	3
Whole	1 to 1¼ lb. plus 2 T. water	11½ to 13	5
Frozen, flowerets	1 package (10 oz.) plus 1 T. water	5½ to 7	3
CORN, Whole Kernel Frozen	1 package (10 oz.) plus 1 T. water	4 to 5½	3
CORN, On the cob Fresh (remove husk and silk)	1 ear — plus 2 2 ears — tablespoons 4 ears — water 6 ears —	2 to 3 3 to 4 8½ to 10 13 to 14½	3 3 5 5
Frozen (rinse off any frost)	1 ear 2 ears 4 ears 6 ears	3½ to 4½ 5 to 6½ 9½ to 11 14 to 15½	3 3 5 5
EGGPLANT, Fresh Cubed	1 pound plus 2 T. water	7 to 8½	3
Whole (pierce skin)	1 to 1¼ pounds	4½ to 6	3
LIMA BEANS Frozen	1 package (10 oz.) plus ½ T. water	5½ to 7	3

FRESH AND FROZEN VEGETABLE CHART FOR TIME COOKING

VEGETABLES	AMOUNT	APPROX. COOKING TIME, covered, at HIGH (in minutes)	STAND TIME (in minutes)
OKRA, Frozen Sliced Whole	1 package (10 oz.) plus 1 T. water 1 package (10 oz.) plus 1 T. water	5 to 6½ 5½ to 7	3 3
ONIONS Fresh, (small, whole)	8 to 10 plus 2 T. water (about 1 lb.)	6½ to 8	3
PEAS, GREEN Fresh Frozen	1½ pounds plus 3 T. water 1 package (10 oz.) plus 1 T. water	5 to 6½ 5½ to 7	3 3
PEAS, Snow (Pea pods) Frozen	1 package (6 oz.) plus 1 T. water	4½ to 5½	3
PEAS and CARROTS Frozen	1 package (10 oz.) plus 1 T. water	5½ to 7	3
PEAS, Black-eyed Frozen	1 package (10 oz.) plus ½ cup water	15 to 18	5
POTATOES* Fresh, whole for baking	1 (about 6 oz. ea.) 2 4 6	4½ to 5½ 7 to 9 10 to 12 14 to 16	3 to 5 3 to 5 3 to 5 3 to 5
SPINACH Fresh, leaf Frozen, leaf or chopped	1 pound plus 2 T. water 1 package (10 oz.) plus 1 T. water	5½ to 7 6½ to 8	3 3
SQUASH (Summer), sliced ½-in. thick Fresh Frozen	1 pound plus 2 T. water 1 package (10 oz.) plus 1 T. water	6½ to 8 5 to 6½	3 3
SQUASH (Winter) Fresh, whole (pierce skin) Frozen, whipped	1 (1 lb.) 2 (¾ lb. ea.) 1 package (12 oz.) plus 1 T. water	6 to 7½ 7½ to 9 6½ to 8	5 5 3
SUCCOTASH Frozen	1 package (10 oz.) plus 1 T. water	5½ to 7	3
VEGETABLES, mixed Frozen	1 package (10 oz.) plus 1 T. water	6½ to 8	3
ZUCCHINI, sliced ½-in. thick Fresh Frozen	1 pound plus 2 T. water 1 package (10 oz.) plus 1 T. water	6½ to 8 5 to 6½	3 3

Potatoes can be wrapped in aluminum foil after heating to keep warm for serving.

MASHED POTATOES I-M

6 medium potatoes (about 2 pounds),
  peeled and quartered
½ to ¾ cup milk
¼ cup butter or margarine
Salt and pepper to taste

Yield: 6 Servings

Rinse potatoes; drain. Arrange potatoes in medium glass bowl. Cover completely with plastic wrap.

TO COOK BY INSTA-MATIC: Cook on **COOK 5.** When time appears in display window, stir once.

TO COOK BY TIME: Cook at **HIGH** 9 to 10½ minutes; stir once.

TO COMPLETE: After cooking, release plastic wrap. Potatoes should be tender. Let stand, covered, 5 minutes. Drain. Meanwhile, in large glass bowl, combine remaining ingredients. Cook at **MEDIUM** 2 to 3 minutes, or until hot. Add potatoes and mash until smooth.

Note: For INSTANT mashed potatoes, follow package directions. Cook water, milk and salt in glass bowl at **HIGH** *(see Heating Liquids chart page 56). Stir in butter and instant potato flakes.*

POTATO DUMPLINGS

2 quarts hot water or broth
2 cups hot mashed potatoes
½ cup flour
1 egg
½ teaspoon salt
¼ teaspoon parsley flakes
⅛ teaspoon pepper
Dash nutmeg

Yield: 4–6 Servings

In 3-quart casserole, heat water, covered with lid, at **HIGH** 10 minutes, or until water is boiling.
Meanwhile, combine remaining ingredients; drop by heaping tablespoons into water. Cook at **HIGH** 3 to 4 minutes or until dumplings float; drain.

SWEET POTATO PONE

¼ cup butter or margarine
2 cans (16 oz. ea.) sweet potatoes or yams,
  drained
1 egg
½ cup milk
2 tablespoons packed brown sugar
2 tablespoons molasses
½ teaspoon cinnamon
¼ teaspoon nutmeg
Dash cloves
½ cup miniature marshmallows, optional

Yield: 6 Servings

Heat butter in 1½-quart casserole at **HIGH** 1 to 1½ minutes, or until melted. In medium bowl, combine butter, sweet potatoes, egg, milk, sugar, molasses, cinnamon, nutmeg and cloves; mash until smooth. Spread into same casserole dish; cover with plastic wrap. Cook at **HIGH** 8 to 9 minutes, or until heated through.
Top with marshmallows. Cook, uncovered, at **HIGH** ½ minute.

SWISS SCALLOPED CORN

3 slices bacon, diced
2 cans (17 oz.) whole kernel corn, drained
1 cup (4 oz.) shredded Swiss cheese
½ teaspoon onion powder
⅛ teaspoon pepper
1½ tablespoons flour
1 egg
1 can (5⅓ oz.) evaporated milk
¼ cup dry bread crumbs
1 tablespoon butter or margarine, melted
Paprika

Yield: 6 Servings

In medium glass bowl, cook bacon at **HIGH** 2 to 3 minutes, or until crisp. Drain all but 1 tablespoon fat. Stir in corn, cheese, onion powder, pepper and flour blended with egg and milk. Pour into a 2-quart glass ring mold. Top with bread crumbs blended with butter and paprika. Cook at **MEDIUM** 11 to 14 minutes or until set. Let stand, covered, 5 minutes before serving.

Variation: Use 1 cup (4 oz.) shredded Chedder cheese in place of Swiss Cheese.

PASTAS, GRAINS and CEREALS

To tempt you into trying rice, pasta and cereals in the microwave oven, here are delicious recipes you will not be able to resist. Microwave cooked pasta and rice will eliminate sticky pans. Microwaved hot cereals are cooked directly in the cereal bowl and makes clean-up easy.

COOKING RICE AND OTHER GRAINS

ITEM	CONTAINER	AMOUNT OF HOT WATER	APPROX. TIME TO BOIL WATER at HIGH (in minutes)	APPROX. TIME TO COOK GRAIN at MEDIUM-LOW (in minutes)	STAND TIME (in minutes)
RICE Brown (1 cup)	2-qt. casserole	3 cups	5 to 6	45 to 50	15
Flavored Rice Mix (6 oz.)	2-qt. casserole	as package directs	4 to 5	20	10
Long Grain (1 cup)	2-qt. casserole	2 cups	4 to 5	14 to 16	10
Long Grain & Wild Rice Mix (6 oz.)	2-qt. casserole	2 cups	4½ to 5	23 to 25	5
Quick Rice (1 cup)	1-qt. casserole	1 cup	2 to 3	5	5
Short Grain (1 cup)	2-qt. casserole	2 cups	4 to 5	10 to 12	10
BARLEY Quick Cook (1 cup)	2-qt. casserole	3 cups	5 to 6	5½ to 6½	3 (then drain)
GRITS (⅔ cup)	3-qt. casserole	3⅓ cups	5 to 6	10	10

COOKING RICE BY INSTA-MATIC I-M

ITEM	CONTAINER	AMOUNT OF COLD WATER	INSTA-MATIC CYCLE
Long Grain, regular (1 cup)	2-qt. casserole	2 cups	COOK 3
Long Grain, Enriched, Parboiled (1 cup)	2-qt. casserole	2½ cups	COOK 3
Flavored Rice Mix (6 oz.)	2-qt. casserole	as package directs	COOK 2
Long Grain and Wild Rice Mix (6 oz.)	2-qt. casserole	2½ cups	COOK 2

NOTE: Brown Rice is not suitable for INSTA-MATIC Cooking.

SPANISH RICE

1 large onion, chopped
¼ cup finely chopped green pepper
2 tablespoons butter or margarine
Water
1 can (16 oz.) stewed tomatoes, chopped
   and drained; reserve liquid
1 cup long grain rice
1½ teaspoons salt
⅛ teaspoon pepper

Yield: 6 Servings

In 2-quart casserole, combine onion, green pepper and butter. Cook at **HIGH** 2½ to 3½ minutes; stir once. Add enough water to reserved liquid to equal 2 cups. Add to dish with tomatoes, rice, salt and pepper. Cook, covered with lid, at **HIGH** 4 to 5 minutes and at **MEDIUM-LOW** 16 to 17 minutes, or until rice is tender; stir once. Let stand, covered, 5 minutes before serving.

RICE PILAF

¼ cup butter or margarine
1 cup long grain rice
2 cups chicken broth
¼ cup raisins, optional
1 to 1½ teaspoons curry powder

Yield: 6 Servings

Heat butter in 2-quart casserole at **MEDIUM-LOW** 1 minute, or until melted; stir in rice. Heat at **HIGH** 2 to 3 minutes, or until rice is browned; stir once. Add remaining ingredients and cook covered, with lid, at **HIGH** 5 minutes and at **MEDIUM-LOW** 12 to 14 minutes, or until rice is tender. Let stand, covered, 5 minutes.

Variation: Cook ¼ cup slivered almonds with butter.

HOPPIN' JOHN

4 slices bacon, diced
1 medium onion, chopped
2 cups hot water
1½ cups cooked black-eyed peas
1 cup long grain rice
1 teaspoon salt
¼ teaspoon pepper
Dash hot pepper sauce, optional

Yield: 6 Servings

Combine bacon and onion in 2½-quart casserole. Cook at **HIGH** 4 to 5 minutes, or until bacon is crisp; stir once. Stir in remaining ingredients. Cook, covered, with lid, at **HIGH** 5 minutes and at **MEDIUM-LOW** 12 to 14 minutes, or until rice is tender; stir once. Let stand, covered, 5 minutes before serving.

BARLEY MUSHROOM CASSEROLE

6 tablespoons butter or margarine
2 medium onions, finely chopped
3 cloves garlic, finely chopped
1 pound fresh mushroom, sliced
1 cup quick cooking barley
½ cup chicken broth
¼ cup chopped parsley
2 teaspoons basil
1 teaspoon salt
¼ teaspoon pepper

Yield: 6 Servings

In 2½-quart casserole, combine butter, onion and garlic. Cook, covered with lid, at **HIGH** 3 to 4 minutes, or until onion is tender. Stir in remaining ingredients. Cook, covered, at **HIGH** 5 minutes and at **MEDIUM-LOW** 5½ to 6½ minutes, or until barley is tender. Let stand, covered, 5 minutes before serving.

DIRECTIONS FOR PREPARING HOT CEREAL

Follow directions in chart for recommended dish size, amount of water, cooking time and power level. Combine cereal and hot water in dish. For Cream of Wheat and Farina, add cereal to boiling water.

Cook; stir once halfway through cooking time.

Let stand 1 to 2 minutes before serving. Top as desired with sugar or spices.

CEREAL	CONTAINER	AMOUNT OF HOT WATER	AMOUNT OF CEREAL	APPROX. COOKING TIME (in minutes)		STAND TIME (in minutes)
				at HIGH	at MEDIUM	
Cream of Wheat 1 serving 2 servings 4 servings	2-cup glass bowl 1-qt. glass bowl 2-qt. glass bowl	1¼ cups 2 cups 3¾ cups	2½ tablespoons ⅓ cup ⅔ cup	1 1½ 2	4 to 6 6 to 7 7 to 8	1 1 2
Farina 1 serving 2 servings 4 servings	individual serving dish 2 individual serving dishes 1-qt. glass bowl	⅔ cup 1⅓ cups 2⅔ cups	2 tablespoons ¼ cup ½ cup	1½ to 2 3¼ to 3¾ 4½ to 5½	—— —— ——	1 1 2
Oatmeal (Quick) 1 serving 2 servings 4 servings	individual serving dish 2 individual serving dishes 1-qt. glass bowl	¾ cup 1½ cups 3 cups	⅓ cup ⅔ cup 1⅓ cups	1 to 1½ 2 to 2½ 3½ to 4	—— —— ——	1 1 2
Wheat-Bran Cereal 1 serving 2 servings 4 servings	individual serving dish 2 individual serving dishes 2-qt. glass bowl	¾ cup 1½ cups 3 cups	¼ cup ½ cup 1 cup	3 5 to 6 7 to 8	—— —— ——	1 1 2

GRANOLA CEREAL

2 cups quick or old fashion oats
⅔ cup soy nuts or coarsely chopped nuts
⅓ cup wheat germ, optional
¼ cup packed brown sugar
¼ cup honey
1 teaspoon vanilla
⅓ cup raisins or coconut

Yield: 3 Cups

Cook oats in 12×8-inch dish at **HIGH** 3 to 5 minutes; stir occasionally. Add nuts, wheat germ, and brown sugar; stir in honey and vanilla. Cook at **HIGH** 3 to 5 minutes; stir twice; add raisins.
Cool completely, stirring occasionally to crumble mixture. Store in airtight container.

Note: *To make GRANOLA SNACK, follow above procedure. Add ¼ cup oil with honey.*

NICE AND SPICY OATMEAL

4 cups hot water
2 cups quick-cooking oats
½ cup chopped dried apricots or raisins
¼ cup packed brown sugar
¼ teaspoon salt
½ cup wheat germ, optional
1 teaspoon cinnamon

Yield: 4 Servings

In 2-quart casserole, combine water, oats, apricots, sugar and salt. Cook at **HIGH** 4 to 5 minutes, or until slightly thickened; stir once. Stir in wheat germ and cinnamon. Let stand 3 minutes before serving.

QUICK BREADS

Now, you do not have to get up hours before everyone else to surprise them with a freshly baked treat or plan in advance for something to serve with coffee.

Your microwave oven brings you flexibility for spur of the moment fun. Most breads and coffee cakes bake in 15 to 20 minutes, muffins or buns in about 6 minutes.

DIRECTIONS FOR QUICK BREADS

Prepare batter according to package or recipe directions.

Use recommended dish size. Glass dishes allow bottom of baked goods to be checked visually for doneness. After cooking visually check bottom for doneness.

Grease bottom of dish when cakes are served from the dish. Grease bottom and sides and line bottom of dish with wax paper when the product is inverted and removed from dish. Never flour the dish.

When necessary, shield ends of loaf dishes with 3-inch strip of foil. Shield square dishes with triangle of foil on each corner; mold around dish.

When cooking muffins, line microwave muffin pans with paper baking cups. Fill paper baking cups ⅔ full.

Rotate dish ¼ turn two to three times during cooking. A ¼ turn means that the front and back of the dish becomes the sides.

Check during cooking since brands and cooking times vary. After cooking, tops may be sticky, but a toothpick inserted near center should come out clean.

Let stand, uncovered, on a flat surface for 5 to 15 minutes. Stand time is important to allow product to finish baking

Cakes and breads that are to be inverted should be loosened from the sides of the dish. Carefully turn product out of dish and peel off wax paper. Store, covered, until ready to serve.

QUICK BREAD MIX CHART

Most package mixed and some recipes benefit from 2-stage heating. We have given 2-stage heating directions where they are helpful.

ITEM	AMOUNT OF BATTER	DISH SIZE/ PREPARATION	FIRST STAGE	→ SECOND STAGE	SPECIAL INSTRUCTIONS	STAND TIME
Coffee Cake Fruit Variety (16 to 19 oz.)	All batter	Grease 8 or 9-inch round dish.	**LOW** 6 minutes	→ **MEDIUM-HIGH** 4 to 5½ minutes	Rotate ¼ turn every 5 minutes. To dry top, cover with wax paper during last minute of cooking.	10 minutes, uncovered
Coffee Cake Streusel Variety (10.5 oz.)	All batter	Grease 8 or 9-inch round or square dish.	**LOW** 6 minutes	→ **MEDIUM-HIGH** 2½ to 3 minutes	Shield each corner of square dish with a triangle of foil	10 minutes, uncovered
Quick Bread (14½ to 17 oz.)	All batter	Grease 9×5×3-inch loaf dish. Line bottom with wax paper.	**LOW** 10 minutes	→ **MEDIUM-HIGH** 3½ to 4 minutes	Shield each end with a 3-inch strip of foil. Mold foil around handle. Rotate ¼ turn every 4 minutes.	15 minutes, uncovered
Corn Bread (10 to 12 oz.)	All batter	Grease 8 or 9-inch round or square dish.	**LOW** 6 minutes	→ **MEDIUM-HIGH** 2½ to 3½ minutes	Increase milk by 8 Tbsp. Add 1 Tbsp. oil to batter. Shield each corner of square dish with a triangle of foil. Mold foil around dish. Rotate ¼ turn every 4 minutes.	10 minutes, uncovered
Gingerbread (14 oz.)	All batter	Grease 8-inch square dish.	**MEDIUM** 8 minutes	_____	_____	15 minutes, uncovered
Muffins (cook 6 at a time)	Scant ¼ cup per muffin	6-cup muffin pan lined with paper baking cups.	**MEDIUM-LOW** 4½ to 5½ minutes	_____	_____	5 minutes, uncovered

IRISH SODA BREAD

2 cups flour
2 tablespoons sugar
½ teaspoon salt
½ teaspoon baking powder
3 tablespoons butter or margarine
1 cup raisins
2 tablespoons caraway seeds
¾ cup buttermilk
1 egg
½ teaspoon baking soda

Yield: 6 Servings

Sift together flour, sugar, salt and baking powder; cut in butter. Stir in raisins and caraway. Combine buttermilk, egg and baking soda; add to dry ingredients, stirring only until flour is moistened. On floured board, lightly knead dough until smooth, about ½ minute. Shape into ball and place in 1½-quart casserole, bottom lined with wax paper; cut an "X" across top of dough. Cook at **MEDIUM** 7 to 9 minutes. Let stand, uncovered, 10 minutes; turn out of casserole. Let stand upside down an additional 10 minutes; cool completely; store, covered, until ready to serve.

BASIC NUT BREAD

½ cup packed brown sugar
3 tablespoons butter or margarine
2 eggs
¾ cup buttermilk
½ teaspoon vanilla
1¼ cups flour
¾ cup chopped nuts
1½ teaspoons baking powder
½ teaspoon cinnamon
½ teaspoon salt
Cinnamon sugar

Yield: 1 Loaf

Cream together sugar and butter; stir in eggs, buttermilk and vanilla. Add flour, nuts, baking powder, cinnamon, and salt, stirring only until flour is moistened. Spoon batter into 9"×5"×3" greased glass loaf dish, bottom lined with wax paper. Sprinkle with cinnamon sugar. Shield ends of dish with 3-inch strip of foil, mold foil around dish. Cook at **LOW** 10 minutes and at **MEDIUM-HIGH** 3 to 5 minutes, or until toothpick inserted near center comes out clean. Let stand, uncovered, 15 minutes. Invert and remove wax paper; let stand 5 minutes. Store, covered, until ready to serve.

BOSTON BROWN BREAD

1 cup buttermilk
½ cup molasses
½ cup raisins
½ teaspoon baking powder
½ teaspoon baking soda
½ teaspoon salt
½ cup whole wheat flour
½ cup yellow cornmeal
¼ cup flour

Yield: 1 Loaf

Combine buttermilk and molasses; stir in raisins, baking powder, baking soda and salt. Add flours and cornmeal, stir only until moistened. Pour batter into generously greased 4 cup-glass measure. Cover loosely with plastic wrap; hold wrap in place with rubber band secured under handle of glass measure. Place on inverted pie plate in oven. Cook at **MEDIUM** 8 to 9 minutes. Let stand, uncovered, 10 minutes. Remove from dish; let stand 5 minutes. Store, covered, until ready to serve.

196

SIESTA CORNBREAD

1 package (12 oz.) corn muffin mix
½ cup chopped onion
2 tablespoons chopped pimento
1 to 2 tablespoons chopped jalapeno
   peppers
1 can (8¼ oz.) cream-style corn
1 egg
¼ cup milk
2 tablespoons oil

Yield: 6 Servings

Combine corn muffin mix, onion, pimento and peppers; stir in corn, egg, milk and oil. Spoon batter into greased 2-quart ring mold. Cook at **LOW** 6 minutes and **MEDIUM-HIGH** 5 to 6 minutes or until bread pulls away from center and sides of dish. Let stand, 10 minutes. Invert from dish and serve warm.

SOUTHERN CHEESE SPOON BREAD

½ cup yellow cornmeal
2 cups milk
½ teaspoon salt
2 eggs, beaten
1 cup (4 oz.) diced American cheese
2 tablespoons butter or margarine

Yield: 6 Servings

In medium glass bowl, combine cornmeal, milk and salt. Heat at **HIGH** 3 minutes and at **MEDIUM** 3 to 4 minutes or until cornmeal is thickened; stir twice. Stir until smooth; and eggs, cheese and butter. Stir until cheese and butter are almost melted. Pour into greased 1-quart casserole. Cook covered with glass lid, at **MEDIUM** 2 minutes. Stir well; recover. Cook at **MEDIUM** 5 minutes, or until center is almost set. Let stand 10 minutes before serving.

PECAN STICKY BUNS

½ cup packed brown sugar
⅓ cup finely chopped pecans
1 teaspoon cinnamon
¼ cup butter or margarine, melted
1 can (8 oz.) refrigerated crescent dinner
   rolls

Yield: 8 Buns

In small bowl, combine sugar, pecans and cinnamon. Unroll the 2 sections of dough, but do not separate. On each long rectangle, brush on 1 teaspoon butter and spoon 2 tablespoons pecan mixture; re-roll. Cut each into quarters, forming 8 buns. Dip each bun into butter and then into pecan mixture. In 8-inch round dish, arrange biscuits in ring (do not place any in center); sprinkle remaining pecan mixture over ring. Cook at **MEDIUM** 4½ to 5½ minutes. Let stand, covered, 5 minutes before inverting onto platter. Cover until ready to serve.

CHERRY BRUNCH ROLLS

½ cup packed brown sugar
¼ cup chopped maraschino cherries
¼ cup flaked coconut
1 tablespoon water
¼ teaspoon cinnamon
1 can (8 oz.) refrigerated biscuits
3 tablespoons butter or margarine, melted

Yield: 10 Rolls

In small glass bowl, combine brown sugar, cherries, coconut, water and cinnamon. Stir until smooth. Cook at **HIGH** 2 to 2¼ minutes. Pour into a greased 5-cup ring mold. Dip each biscuit into melted butter. Arrange biscuits on top of cherry mixture. Cook at **MEDIUM** 4 to 4½ minutes. Let stand, covered, 5 minutes before inverting on serving platter. Store, covered, until ready to serve.

PUMPKIN PECAN MUFFINS

1 cup flour
⅔ cup sugar
1¼ teaspoons pumpkin pie spice
1 teaspoon baking powder
⅛ teaspoon salt
½ cup chopped nuts
½ cup raisins
½ cup cooked pumpkin
¼ cup milk
3 tablespoons oil
1 egg, beaten

Yield: 12 Muffins

Combine flour, sugar, pumpkin pie spice, baking powder and salt. Stir in nuts and raisins. Add pumpkin, milk, oil and egg; stir until flour is moistened. Line 6-cup muffin pan with paper baking cups; fill ¾ full. Cook at **MEDIUM-LOW** 5½ to 6½ minutes, or until toothpick inserted near center comes out clean. Rotate dish ¼ turn halfway through cooking. Let stand 5 minutes. Repeat procedure with remaining batter. Store covered.

EASY MORNING MUFFINS

2 cups flour
½ cup sugar
1 tablespoon baking powder
½ teaspoon salt
½ cup milk
½ cup oil
2 eggs, beaten
3 tablespoons butter or margarine, melted
Cinnamon sugar

Yield: 12 Muffins

Combine flour, sugar, baking powder and salt. Add milk, oil and eggs; stir until flour is moistened. Line 6-cup muffin pan with paper baking cups; fill ¾ full. Cook at **MEDIUM-LOW** 4½ to 5½ minutes, or until toothpick inserted near center comes out clean. Rotate dish ¼ turn halfway through cooking. Let stand 5 minutes. Repeat procedure with remaining batter. If desired, dip tops of muffins in melted butter and then in cinnamon sugar. Store covered.

Variations: Add any ½ cup of the following, tossed with 1 tablespoon flour.
  ● *Blueberries*
  ● *Chopped nuts*
  ● *Raisins*

198

RAISIN BRAN MUFFINS

2¼ cups raisin bran cereal
⅔ cup milk
6 tablespoons oil
2 eggs, beaten
⅔ cup flour
6 tablespoons packed brown sugar
1 tablespoon baking powder
½ teaspoon cinnamon

Yield: 12 Muffins

Combine cereal, milk, oil and eggs. Stir until cereal is moistened. Let stand 5 minutes. Combine flour, sugar, baking powder and cinnamon. Add to cereal mixture; stir until well blended. Line 6-cup muffin pan with paper baking cups; fill ¾ full. Cook at **MEDIUM-LOW** 5½ to 6½ minutes, or until toothpick inserted near center comes out clean. Rotate dish ¼ turn halfway through cooking. Let stand 5 minutes. Repeat procedure with remaining batter. Serve warm.

PEACHY MUFFINS

1 can (8¾ oz.) sliced peaches, drained; reserve ¼ cup liquid
⅓ cup packed brown sugar
3 tablespoons butter or margarine
1 egg, beaten
¼ cup milk
1 cup flour
½ cup chopped pecans
1½ teaspoons baking powder
½ teaspoon salt
½ teaspoon nutmeg

Yield: 12 Muffins

Finely chop peaches; set aside. Cream together sugar and butter. Stir in egg, milk and reserved syrup. Add flour, pecans, baking powder, salt and nutmeg. Stir only until flour is moistened. Stir in peaches. Line 6-cup muffin pan with paper baking cups; fill ¾ full. Cook at **MEDIUM-LOW** 5½ to 6½ minutes, or until toothpick inserted near center comes out clean. Rotate dish ¼ turn halfway through cooking. Let stand 5 minutes. Repeat procedure with remaining batter. Store covered.

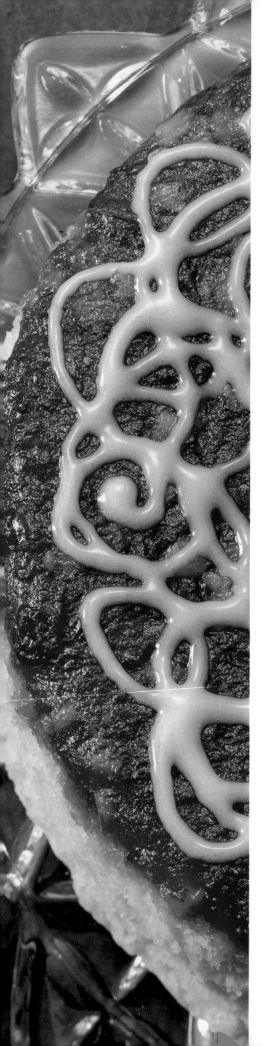

HOLIDAY CRANBERRY COFFEE CAKE

1 can (8 oz.) whole berry cranberry sauce
6 tablespoons sugar, divided
¼ cup chopped nuts, optional
1 tablespoon butter or margarine, melted
2 cups buttermilk biscuit mix
1 cup orange juice or apple juice
1 egg

Glaze:
1 cup confectioners sugar
1 to 2 tablespoons water
½ teaspoon vanilla

Yield: 8 Servings

In small bowl, combine cranberry sauce, 4 tablespoons sugar, nuts and butter. Cook at **HIGH** 2 minutes. Spread into 8 or 9-inch round baking dish, bottom lined with wax paper. Combine biscuit mix, juice, egg and remaining sugar; blend until smooth, about ½ minute. Spoon batter over cranberry mixture. Cover with wax paper. Cook at **LOW** 8 minutes and at **MEDIUM-HIGH** 3½ to 4½ minutes, or until toothpick inserted near center comes out clean. Let stand, uncovered, 10 minutes before inverting onto platter; carefully peel off wax paper. Store cake, covered, until ready to serve.
Meanwhile, prepare glaze. In bowl, combine sugar, water and vanilla; stir until smooth. Drizzle with glaze just before serving.

SOUR CREAM COFFEE CAKE

½ cup sugar
¼ cup butter or margarine
1½ cups flour
1 cup sour cream
2 eggs
1½ teaspoons vanilla
1 teaspoon baking powder
1 teaspoon baking soda
½ teaspoon salt

Topping:
⅓ cup chopped walnuts
¼ cup sugar
½ teaspoon cinnamon

Yield: 8 Servings

Cream sugar and butter in large bowl, with electric mixer. Add remaining ingredients. Beat at low speed 30 seconds and at medium speed 2 minutes. Pour into greased 8-inch square dish. In small bowl, combine topping ingredients; sprinkle over batter. Shield each corner of dish with a triangle of foil; mold foil around dish. Cook at **LOW** 8 minutes and at **MEDIUM-HIGH** 3 to 4 minutes. Rotate dish ¼ turn every 5 minutes. Let stand 10 minutes. Serve immediately.

GRAHAM STREUSEL COFFEE I-M CAKE

½ cup butter or margarine, melted
1 cup graham cracker crumbs
½ cup packed brown sugar
⅓ cup chopped nuts
¾ teaspoon cinnamon
1 package (18¼ oz.) yellow cake mix
4 eggs
1 cup water
⅓ cup oil

Vanilla Glaze:
2 cups confectioners sugar
2 to 3 tablespoons water
1 teaspoon vanilla

Yield: 10 Servings

In medium bowl, combine butter, crumbs, sugar, nuts and cinnamon. Divide crumb mixture into two 8 or 9-inch round baking dishes, bottoms lined with wax paper. Spread to cover bottom of dishes. In large bowl, with electric mixer, blend cake mix, eggs, water and oil at low speed ½ minute; beat at medium speed 3 minutes. Pour 2 cups batter into each dish.

TO COOK BY INSTA-MATIC: Cover completely with plastic wrap. Cook on **COOK 7**.

TO COOK BY TIME: Cook at **LOW** 6 minutes and at **MEDIUM-HIGH** 2 to 3 minutes, or until toothpick inserted near center comes out clean.

TO COMPLETE: Let stand, uncovered, 10 minutes. Repeat procedure with remaining cake.
Meanwhile, prepare glaze. In bowl, combine sugar, water and vanilla; stir until smooth. With knife, loosen cake from sides of dish. Invert one cake onto serving platter; carefully peel off wax paper. Invert second layer onto paper plate; carefully peel off wax paper. Cover until cool; just before serving spread half of glaze on cake on serving platter; top with second layer. Drizzle with remaining glaze.

BANANA NUT COFFEE CAKE I-M

¼ cup oil
¼ cup milk
1 egg
½ cup mashed ripe banana (about 1)
½ cup packed brown sugar
¾ cup flour
½ cup chopped nuts
¾ teaspoon baking powder
¼ teaspoon salt
¼ teaspoon baking soda

Nut Topping:
¼ cup packed brown sugar
¼ cup chopped nuts
2 tablespoons flour
⅛ teaspoon cinnamon
1 tablespoon butter or margarine, softened

Yield: 8 Servings

In medium bowl, combine oil, milk, egg, banana and sugar; add flour, nuts, baking powder, salt and baking soda. Stir only until flour is moistened. Pour into greased 8 or 9-inch round baking dish.
Combine brown sugar, nuts, flour and cinnamon. Blend in butter. Sprinkle on top of coffee cake.

TO COOK BY INSTA-MATIC: Cover dish completely with plastic wrap. Cook on **COOK 4**.

TO COOK BY TIME: Cook at **MEDIUM** 7½ to 9 minutes, or until toothpick inserted near center comes out clean. Rotate dish ¼ turn halfway through cooking.

TO COMPLETE: Let stand, uncovered, 10 minutes. Store, covered, until ready to serve.

201

2-STAGE MICROWAVE DEFROSTING AND RISING OF FROZEN BREAD DOUGH

1. Fill a 11¾×7½-inch glass baking dish with 2 cups hot tap water. Heat at **HIGH** 2 minutes.
2. Generously grease one or two 8×4-inch glass loaf dishes and all sides of bread dough. Place dough in loaf dish; set in hot water. Cover with wax paper.
3. Heat at **MEDIUM-LOW**, 2 minutes.
4. Turn dough over and rotate dish ¼ turn.
5. Heat at **HIGH**, 2 minutes.
6. Let stand in oven 10 minutes. Dough should be defrosted and slightly warm. If needed, continue heating at **HIGH** in 1 minute intervals, until defrosted.
7. Heat at **MEDIUM-LOW**, 1 minute. Let stand in oven 15 minutes. Rearrange dishes after stand time. Repeat procedure until dough rises 1-inch above dish.
   (Preheat conventional oven during time bread is standing. Dough should remain in microwave oven until ready to bake or it may fall.)
8. Bake bread in conventional oven according to package directions.

RISING HOMEMADE YEAST DOUGH

1. Prepare yeast dough according to recipe directions. Do not select a recipe that yields more than 2 loaves.
2. Generously grease a glass bowl that will be large enough to hold dough when doubled in size.
3. Generously grease dough on all sides before placing in bowl; cover with wax paper.
4. Place bowl in a 11¾ or 7½-inch glass baking dish filled with 2 cups hot water. Place in oven.
5. Heat at **MEDIUM-LOW**, 1 minute. Let stand in oven 15 minutes. Repeat procedure until dough has doubled in size. Turn dish ½ turn after each stand time. If surface of dough appears to be drying, carefully turn dough over in bowl.
6. Punch down dough, divide and shape into one or two loaves.
7. Place shaped dough into well greased 8×4-inch glass loaf dishes; set in original dish of hot water. Cover dough with wax paper.
8. Heat at **MEDIUM-LOW**, 1 minute. Let stand 15 minutes. Repeat procedure until dough rises to volume described in recipe. Rearrange dishes after each stand time.
   (Preheat conventional oven during time bread is standing. Dough should remain in microwave oven until ready to bake or it may fall).
9. Bake bread in conventional oven according to package directions.

Note: *If dough is to be baked in any container other than glass, second rising must be done at room temperature.*

DESSERTS and CANDIES

This chapter offers a wide variety of popular dessert recipes; cakes, pies, bar cookies and fruit-type desserts. We have included both recipes from scratch and convenience mixes. Many of these can be cooked during dinner and served warm.

DIRECTIONS FOR CAKES AND CUPCAKES

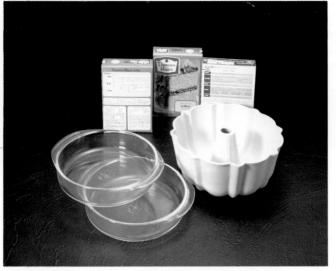

Prepare batter according to package or recipe directions. Layer cakes must be baked one layer at a time. Or, the entire cake mix may be baked in a 12 or 14 cup fluted tube dish.

Use dishes recommended in chart or recipes. Glass baking dishes allow the bottom of the cakes to be checked for doneness. When the product is removed from the oven, visually check bottom.

Grease the bottom of the baking dish when cakes are to be served directly from the dish. Grease the bottom and sides of dish when cake is to be inverted and removed from dish, such as layer cakes, up-side down cakes. If desired, bottom of dish may be lined with wax paper. Never flour cake dishes and fluted tube dishes.

Use only 2¼ cups of batter for an 8 or 9-inch round or square baking dish. Cook second layer immediately after the first. The remaining batter can be used for cupcakes.

When using fluted tube dish, be sure to grease sides and "tube". All the batter from a 2 layer cake mix may be poured into a 12 or 14 cup fluted tube dish.

When necessary, square dishes can be shielded on each corner with a triangle of foil. Mold foil around dish.

When cooking cupcakes, line microwave muffin pans with paper baking cups. Fill paper baking cups half full.

Cover with wax paper when indicated in chart or recipe. Most package mixes and some recipes benefit from 2-stage cooking. We have given 2-stage cooking directions where they are helpful.

For best results, rotate dish ¼ turn two to three times during cooking.
A ¼ turn means that the front and back of the dish becomes the sides.

Check cakes during cooking since brands and cooking times vary. After cooking, tops may be sticky, but a toothpick inserted near center should come out clean.

Let stand, uncovered, on a flat surface for 5 to 15 minutes. Stand time is important to allow cakes and cupcakes to finish cooking.

To invert, loosen cakes from sides of dish. Carefully turn out. Store, covered, until ready to serve. Cool completely to frost. Apply frosting with light pressure.

CAKE MIX CHART

ITEM	AMOUT OF BATTER	DISH SIZE/ PREPARATION	FIRST STAGE →	SECOND STAGE	SPECIAL INSTRUCTIONS	STAND TIME
Cake Mix (18¾ to 20¼ oz.)	2¼ cups	Grease 8 or 9-inch round or square dish.	**LOW** 6 minutes	**MEDIUM-HIGH** 3½ to 4½ minutes	Shield each corner of square dish with triangle of foil. Rotate ¼ turn every 3 minutes.	10 minutes, uncovered
Cake Mix (18¾ to 20¼ oz.)	All batter	Grease 16-cup fluted tube dish.	**LOW** 10 minutes	**MEDIUM-HIGH** 6½ to 7 minutes	Cover dish with wax paper during last minute of cooking. Rotate ¼ turn every 5 minutes.	15 minutes, uncovered
Brownies (15 oz.) Cake-Like	All batter	8 or 9-inch round or square dish.	**MEDIUM** 8 to 9 minutes	———	Shield each corner of square with triangle of foil. Rotate ¼ turn every 3 minutes.	until completely cool
Cupcakes	2 rounded table-spoons per cup cake	Muffin pan lined with paper baking cups 1 2 4 6	**MEDIUM** ½ to 1 1 to 1¼ 2 to 2½ 3 to 4 minutes	———	Place muffin pan on inverted pie plate.	5 minutes, uncovered
Mix-in-Dish Cake (15 oz.) No frosting	All batter	Grease 8 or 9-inch round or square dish.	**LOW** 8 minutes	**MEDIUM-HIGH** 3½ to 4 minutes	Shield each corner of square dish with triangle of foil. Rotate ¼ turn every 4 minutes. Cover dish with wax paper last minute of cooking.	10 minutes, uncovered
Mix-in-Dish Cake (11.4 oz.) with frosting	All batter	Cardboard pan provided with mix.	**LOW** 5 minutes	**MEDIUM-HIGH** 1½ to 2 minutes	———	until cool, uncovered

CARROT SPICE CAKE **I-M**

1¼ cups flour
1 cup packed brown sugar
1 teaspoon baking powder
1 teaspoon baking soda
2 teaspoons cinnamon
½ teaspoon allspice
½ teaspoon salt
1¼ cups shredded carrot
⅔ cup oil
2 eggs
1 can (8 oz.) crushed pineapple, drained
1 teaspoon vanilla
½ cup chopped nuts
¼ cup raisins

Yield: 8 Servings

In large bowl, with electric mixer, combine flour, sugar, baking powder, baking soda, cinnamon, allspice, salt and carrot. Stir in oil, eggs, pineapple and vanilla and beat 2 minutes at medium speed. Stir in nuts and raisins. Pour batter into a greased 10 to 12 cup fluted tube dish.

TO COOK BY INSTA-MATIC: Cover completely with 2 pieces of plastic wrap. Cook on **COOK 3.**

TO COOK BY TIME: Cover with wax paper. Cook at **MEDIUM** 10 to 11 minutes, or until toothpick inserted near center comes out clean.

TO COMPLETE: Let stand, uncovered, 10 minutes. Store, covered, until ready to serve.

YELLOW CAKE

¾ cup sugar
⅓ cup butter or margarine
1 egg
⅔ cup milk
1 teaspoon vanilla
1 cup flour
1½ teaspoons baking powder
¼ teaspoon salt

Yield: 1 Layer

Cream sugar and butter in large bowl, with electric mixer. Add egg, milk and vanilla, mixing until blended. Stir in remaining ingredients. Beat 1 minute at medium speed. Grease an 8 or 9-inch round baking dish with wax paper. Pour batter into dish; cover with wax paper. Elevate dish, in oven, on inverted glass saucer. Cook at **LOW** 6 minutes. Rotate dish ¼ turn after 3 minutes. Cook at **MEDIUM-HIGH** 2½ to 3½ minutes, or until toothpick inserted near center comes out clean. Let stand, uncovered, 15 minutes. Invert on serving plate; peel off wax paper. Store covered.

CHOCOLATE POUND CAKE

1 package (18½ oz.) chocolate cake mix*
1 package (4½ oz.) instant chocolate
　pudding mix*
4 eggs
1¼ cups water
⅓ cup oil

Yield: 12 Servings

In large bowl, combine all ingredients; with electric mixer, beat at medium speed 2 minutes. Pour batter into greased 16-cup fluted tube dish. Cook at **LOW** 10 minutes, and at **MEDIUM-HIGH** 6 to 7 minutes, or until toothpick inserted near center comes out clean. Rotate dish ¼ turn every 5 minutes. To dry top, cover with wax paper during last 1 minute of cooking.
Let stand, uncovered, 15 minutes before inverting onto serving plate; let stand, until cool. Store covered.

*_**Variation:** Use yellow cake mix and instant lemon pudding mix for chocolate cake and pudding mixes. Reduce water to 1 cup._

FESTIVE RUM CAKE

1 cup finely chopped pecans or walnuts
1 package (18¼ oz.) yellow cake mix
1 package (3¾ oz.) instant vanilla pudding
mix
4 eggs
½ cup water
½ cup oil
½ cup dark rum

Rum Glaze:
½ cup butter or margarine, melted
1 cup sugar
¼ cup water
¼ cup ⅓ cup dark rum

Yield: 12 Servings

Sprinkle nuts in well-greased 16 cup fluted tube dish. In large bowl, with electric mixer, combine cake mix, pudding mix, eggs, water, oil and rum; beat at medium speed 4 minutes. Pour batter evenly over nuts.

Cook at **LOW** 10 minutes and at **MEDIUM-HIGH** 6 to 8 minutes or until toothpick inserted near center comes out clean. To dry top of cake, cover with wax paper last 2 minutes of cooking.

Let stand, uncovered, 15 minutes. Meanwhile, in 2-cup measure combine butter, sugar and water; mix well. Cook at **HIGH** 2 to 2½ minutes; stir in rum. Prick top of cake; drizzle half of Rum Glaze over cake (to absorb). Invert cake onto serving platter and prick top and sides of cake; drizzle cake with remaining glaze. Store, covered, until ready to serve.

GERMAN CHOCOLATE I-M
UPSIDE-DOWN CAKE

¾ cup packed brown sugar
3 tablespoons butter or margarine
Pecan halves (about ½ cup)
½ cup flaked coconut
2 tablespoons milk
Single layer chocolate cake mix*
Ingredients as cake package directs

Yield: 8 Servings

Cook sugar and butter in small glass bowl at **HIGH** ½ minute, or until butter is melted. Stir until smooth. Spread butter mixture into 8 or 9-inch round baking dish, bottom lined with wax paper. Arrange pecans on top. Sprinkle with coconut and drizzle with milk.

Prepare cake mix according to package directions; pour over coconut.

TO COOK BY INSTA-MATIC: Cover completely with plastic wrap. Cook on **COOK 3**.

TO COOK BY TIME: Cook at **LOW** 6 minutes and at **MEDIUM-HIGH** 4 to 5 minutes, or until toothpick inserted near center comes out clean.

TO COMPLETE: Let stand, uncovered, 10 minutes. Invert onto serving platter; carefully peel off wax paper. Cool completely. Store covered.

Note: *For HOMEMADE German Chocolate Cake, use Devil's Food Cake recipe (page 210); cook 9 to 10 minutes.*

209

PINEAPPLE UPSIDE-DOWN CAKE

1 cup packed brown sugar
6 tablespoons butter or margarine
Water
1 can (20 oz.) sliced pineapple, drained; reserve syrup
10 maraschino cherries
1 package (18 oz.) yellow cake mix
Ingredients as cake package directs

Yield: 2 Layers

In small glass bowl, cook butter, brown sugar and 2 tablespoons water at **HIGH** 3 to 4 minutes, or until mixture boils 1 minute. In 2 (8 or 9-inch) round baking dishes, spread sugar-butter mixture; arrange pineapple and cherries.
Prepare cake mix according to package directions using reserved syrup as part of water. Pour 2¼ cups of batter into each prepared dish. Cover with wax paper. Cook at **LOW** 6 minutes and at **MEDIUM-HIGH** 3 minutes, or until toothpick inserted near center comes out clean.
Let stand 10 minutes. Repeat with remaining layer. With knife loosen cake from sides of dish, invert onto serving platter. Store covered.

APPLESAUCE CAKE

2 cups flour
1 cup chopped walnuts
3 teaspoons cinnamon
2 teaspoons baking soda
1½ teaspoons salt
1 teaspoon baking powder
1 teaspoon nutmeg
¼ teaspoon cloves
2 cups sugar
½ cup oil
3 eggs
1 jar (15 oz.) applesauce

Yield: 12 Servings

Mix flour, walnuts, cinnamon, baking soda, salt, baking powder, nutmeg and cloves; set aside. In large bowl, with electric mixer, beat sugar, oil and eggs at high speed for 5 minutes. Alternately blend in flour mixture and applesauce; beat until smooth. Pour batter into well greased 16-cup fluted tube dish. Cover with wax paper. Cook at **LOW** 10 minutes and at **MEDIUM-HIGH** 7½ to 9 minutes, or until toothpick inserted in center comes out clean. Rotate dish ¼ turn every 5 minutes. Let stand, uncovered, 15 minutes. Invert onto serving plate.

DEVIL'S FOOD CAKE

¾ cup sugar
⅓ cup shortening
1 egg
⅔ hot water
¾ cup flour
¼ cup unsweetened cocoa
½ teaspoon baking soda
½ teaspoon salt
½ teaspoon vanilla
¼ teaspoon baking powder

Yield: 1 Layer

Cream sugar and shortening in large bowl with electric mixer. Add egg and water. Stir in remaining ingredients and blend until smooth. Pour batter into dish bottom lined with wax paper. Cook at **LOW** 6 minutes and at **MEDIUM-HIGH** 3 to 4 minutes, or until toothpick inserted near center comes out clean.
Let stand 15 minutes. Invert cake from dish and cool completely. Store covered.

PLANTATION COCONUT CAKE

1 package (18¼ oz.) yellow cake mix
1 package (3¾ oz.) instant coconut cream
   or toasted coconut pudding mix or
   instant vanilla pudding mix
4 eggs
1 cup water
⅓ cup oil
1 jar (12 oz.) strawberry or raspberry
   preserves

Creamy Glaze:
1½ cups confectioners sugar
2 to 2½ tablespoons milk
2 tablespoons butter or margarine,
   softened
Flaked coconut

Yield: 8 Servings

In a large bowl, with electric mixer,
combine cake mix, pudding mix, eggs,
water and oil; beat at medium speed 2
minutes. Pour batter into greased 16 cup
fluted tube dish.
Cook at **LOW** 10 minutes and at **MEDIUM-
HIGH** 6 minutes, or until toothpick inserted
near center comes out clean. Rotate cake
¼ turn every 5 minutes. To dry top of cake
cover with wax paper during last minute of
cooking.
Let stand, uncovered, 15 minutes before
inverting on plate. Let stand, until cool.
Store covered.
Meanwhile, prepare glaze. In bowl,
combine sugar, milk and butter; stir until
smooth. Split cake into 3 layers; spread
preserves between layers. Drizzle with
creamy glaze and top with coconut. Store
covered.

CREAMY CHEESECAKE

1 package (8 oz.) cream cheese, softened
½ cup sugar
1 egg
1 teaspoon vanilla
1 cup sour cream
9-inch graham cracker crumb crust, baked
 (see page 223)

Yield: 8 Servings

In medium bowl, combine cream cheese,
sugar, egg and vanilla until smooth; stir in
sour cream. Cook at **MEDIUM** 3½ to 4
minutes; stir twice. Pour cheese mixture
into pie crust. Cook at **MEDIUM-LOW** 4 to
6 minutes, or until center is almost set.
Rotate dish ¼ turn halfway through
cooking. Chill at least 3 hours or overnight.

Variations:
For CHOCOLATE Cheesecake, *add 1 packet
(1 oz.) pre-melted unsweetened chocolate
to cream cheese mixture; increase sugar to
⅔ cup.*
For FRUIT-TOPPED Cheesecake, *top chilled
pie with canned fruit pie filling.*
For PRALINE Cheesecake, *brush top of
chilled pie with maple syrup; garnish with
chopped pecans.*
For PINWHEEL Cheesecake, *cook ½ cup
raspberry jam ½ minute at **HIGH**; swirl
into pie before cooking filling in pie crust.*

211

COCONUT NUT TOPPING FOR CAKE

1 cup evaporated milk
1 cup sugar
½ cup butter or margarine
¼ cup flour
1⅓ cups flaked coconut
1 cup chopped nuts
1 teaspoon vanilla

Yield: 2¼ Cups

In medium glass bowl, combine milk, sugar, butter and flour. Cook at **HIGH** 4½ to 5½ minutes, or until mixture is thickened; stir twice. Add remaining ingredients; cool until spreadable, stir occasionally.

SUPER CHOCOLATE FROSTING

3 squares (1 oz. ea.) semi-sweet chocolate
1 can (14 oz.) sweetened condensed milk
½ teaspoon salt
½ teaspoon vanilla

Yield: 1½ Cups

In medium glass bowl, cook chocolate at **MEDIUM-LOW** 3½ to 4 minutes, or until melted. Stir in milk and salt. Cook at **MEDIUM-LOW** 5 minutes, stirring twice. Stir in vanilla. Cool completely before frosting cake.

CARAMEL CREAM FROSTING

8 caramels
1½ to 2 tablespoons water
1 package (3 oz.) cream cheese, softened (see page 234)
2 cups confectioners sugar

Yield: Frost Single Layer

Combine caramel and 1 tablespoon water in medium glass bowl. Cook at **HIGH** 1½ to 2 minutes; stir until smooth. With electric mixer, blend in cream cheese, then sugar; add ½ to 1 tablespoon water to reach desired consistency.

JAM BARS

¼ cup butter or margarine, softened
¼ cup sugar
1 egg
½ cup flour
¼ cup ground walnuts
½ teaspoon grated lemon peel
¼ teaspoon cinnamon
⅛ teaspoon salt
½ cup raspberry or strawberry jam

Topping:
½ cup flour
¼ cup packed brown sugar
3 tablespoons butter or margarine, softened

Yield: 16 Bars

Cream butter and sugar with electric mixer. Add eggs, flour, walnuts, lemon peel, cinnamon and salt. Mix well. Pat mixture into an 8-inch square dish. Cook at **HIGH** 2½ to 3½ minutes or until center is slightly firm.
Meanwhile, mix together topping ingredients until mixture resembles coarse crumbs. Spread jam on top of baked crust; sprinkle topping over jam. Cook at **HIGH** 3 to 3½ minutes or until jam bubbles around edge. Let stand until cool.

MARBLE BROWNIES

1 package (22½ to 23¾ oz.) fudge brownie mix
Ingredients as brownie package directs for fudge-type brownies
2 packages (3 oz. ea.) cream cheese
2 tablespoons butter or margarine
1 egg
¼ cup sugar
1 tablespoon flour
½ teaspoon vanilla

Yield: 32 Brownies

Prepare fudge-type brownies according to package directions. Spread 1 cup batter into each of 2 greased (8 or 9-inch) square baking dishes. Combine cream cheese and butter in small glass bowl. Cook at **MEDIUM-LOW** 1½ to 2 minutes, or until softened; blend in remaining ingredients. Evenly divide cheese mixture into baking dishes; spoon remaining brownie batter on top. With knife, swirl gently to marble. Shield each corner with triangle of foil; mold foil around dish. Cook **LOW** 6 minutes and at **MEDIUM-HIGH** 5 to 7 minutes, or until set. Repeat procedure with remaining dish.
Let stand, uncovered, until cool. Store, covered, until ready to serve.

213

S'MORES

8 graham cracker squares
2 milk chocolate candy bars (1¼ oz. ea.),
  halved
4 marshmallows

Yield: 4 Cookies

For each cookie, arrange 1 graham cracker in center of paper napkin or paper towel; top with chocolate and marshmallow. Cover with graham cracker and wrap in napkin. Arrange on glass oven tray. Heat at **HIGH** ¾ to 1 minute. Let stand 2 minutes before unwrapping.

CRISPY MARSHMALLOW TREATS

1 package (10 oz.) marshmallows
¼ cup butter or margarine
5 cups toasted rice cereal

Yield: 2½ Dozen

Combine marshmallows and butter in large glass bowl. Cook at **HIGH** 3 to 4 minutes; stir twice. Stir until smooth. Add cereal and stir to coat well.
Press into greased 12×8-inch dish. Cool; cut into squares to serve.

Variation: Stir in 1 cup salted peanuts or raisins with cereal.

NUTTY CHIP CHEWS

¾ cup packed brown sugar
½ cup butter or margarine, softened
(see page 234)
1 egg
1 teaspoon vanilla
1 cup flour
¼ teaspoon baking powder
½ cup chopped nuts
1 cup semi-sweet chocolate pieces, divided

Yield: 16 Bars

With electric mixer, cream sugar and butter; add egg and vanilla. Stir in flour and baking powder until well blended; add nuts and ½ cup chocolate pieces.
Spread batter in 8-inch square dish. Top with remaining chocolate. Cook at **LOW** 6 minutes and **MEDIUM-HIGH** 3½ to 4½ minutes, or until top springs back when lightly pressed. To dry top, cover with wax paper last minute of cooking. Let stand, uncovered, until cool. Store, covered, until ready to serve.

QUICK BAR COOKIES (FROM MIX)

1 package (14 oz.) chocolate chip cookie
  mix
Ingredients as package directs
2 tablespoons water

Yield: 16 Bars

Prepare mix according to package directions. Spread dough into ungreased 8-inch square baking dish. Shield each corner with a triangle of foil; mold foil around dish. Place dish on inverted pie plate. Cook at **LOW** 8 minutes and at **MEDIUM-HIGH** 2½ to 3½ minutes or until toothpick inserted near center comes out clean. Let stand, uncovered, until cool. Store, covered, until ready to serve.

COOKING PUDDING AND PIE FILLING MIXES

In a container twice the volume of the mix, combine ingredients according to package directions.

Cook at MEDIUM according to the time recommended in the chart. Stir twice during cooking time.

Chill before serving. Stir rice and tapioca pudding occasionally. Egg custard, rice pudding and tapioca pudding will thicken as they chill.

ITEM	APPROX. COOKING TIME at MEDIUM (in minutes)
Regular Pudding and Pie Filling 4 servings (3¼ to 4⅛ oz.) 6 servings (4¾ to 5½ oz.)	7½ to 9 11½ to 13
Egg Custard* (3 oz.)	7 to 8½
Rice Pudding* (3¾ oz.)	7½ to 9
Tapioca Pudding* (3½ oz.)	7 to 8½

*Mixture will thicken as it chills.

215

CHILLED CHOCOLATE ALMOND SOUFFLE

1 envelope unflavored gelatin
¾ cup sugar, divided
3 eggs, separated
1 cup milk
2 squares (1 oz. ea.) unsweetened chocolate, melted (see page 233)
¼ teaspoon almond extract
1 cup heavy cream, whipped

Yield: 8 Servings

Mix gelatin and ½ cup sugar in large glass bowl. Stir in egg yolks beaten with milk. Cook at **MEDIUM-LOW** 5 to 6 minutes, or until gelatin is dissolved, stir occasionally. With wire whip, stir in chocolate and almond extract; chill until mixture mounds slightly. Stir occasionally.
Meanwhile, beat egg whites until soft peaks form; gradually add remaining sugar and beat until stiff. Fold in chocolate-almond mixture; fold in whipped cream. Turn into small souffle dish with 2-inch collar or 6-cup bowl and chill until firm. Garnish, if desired, with slivered almonds and additional whipped cream.

SUPERB STRAWBERRY SOUFFLE

Water
2 packages (10 oz. ea.) frozen sliced strawberries in heavy syrup, defrosted and drained (reserve syrup) (see page 35)
4 eggs, separated
2 envelopes unflavored gelatin
6 tablespoons sugar, divided
1 cup heavy cream, whipped

Yield: 6–8 Servings

Add water to reserved syrup to equal 1½ cups; stir in egg yolks. In large glass bowl, mix unflavored gelatin and 4 tablespoons sugar; stir in syrup mixture.
Cook at **MEDIUM** 5 to 6 minutes or until gelatin is dissolved, stir occasionally. Stir in an additional 1 cup cold water.
Chill until mixture mounds slightly, stir occasionally. Fold in strawberries. Beat egg whites until soft peaks form; gradually add remaining sugar and beat until stiff. Fold in gelatin mixture, then whipped cream. Turn into small souffle dish with 3-inch collar or 6 cup bowl; chill until firm.

QUICK RICE PUDDING

3 cups milk
½ cup instant rice
1 package (3 oz.) vanilla pudding and pie filling mix
3 tablespoons raisins*
¼ teaspoon cinnamon or nutmeg*

Yield: 6 Servings

Combine all ingredients in 2-quart glass bowl. Cook, covered with wax paper, at **MEDIUM** 11 to 13 minutes, or until pudding is thickened, stir three times. Chill before serving.

***Variations:** Use 1 tablespoon orange liqueur and ½ cup chopped candied fruit for raisins and cinnamon.*

RAISIN BREAD PUDDING

2 cups milk
¼ cup butter or margarine
5 eggs, beaten
½ cup sugar, divided
1 teaspoon vanilla
4 cups cubed raisin bread
   (about 16 slices)
⅛ teaspoon cinnamon

Yield: 6 Servings

Combine milk and butter in 1-quart glass measure. Cook at **MEDIUM** 4½ to 5½ minutes, or until milk is scalded; quickly stir in eggs, sugar and vanilla.
Meanwhile, arrange bread cubes in 2-quart ring mold. Sprinkle with cinnamon. Pour milk-egg mixture over bread. Cook, covered, with plastic wrap, at **MEDIUM** 16 to 18 minutes, or until pudding is set. Serve warm or chilled.

STEAMED DATE-NUT PUDDING

1¼ cups flour
½ cup each chopped walnuts and dates
½ cup raisins
1 teaspoon cinnamon
½ teaspoon baking soda
½ teaspoon salt
¾ cup hot water
½ cup molasses
1 egg
2 tablespoons butter or margarine, melted

Yield: 8 Servings

In medium bowl, combine flour, walnuts, dates, raisins, cinnamon, baking soda and salt. Stir in water, molasses, egg and butter. Pour batter into a greased 10 cup fluted tube dish or 6 cup fluted glass mold. Cover completely with plastic wrap. Cook at **MEDIUM** 8 to 10 minutes, or until pudding is set.
Release plastic wrap. Let stand, covered, 10 minutes. Invert onto serving platter; serve warm or cover until cool.

BASIC EGG CUSTARD

2 cups milk
4 eggs, beaten
¼ to ⅓ cup sugar
½ teaspoon vanilla
Dash nutmeg

Yield: 6 Servings

Heat milk in 1-quart glass measure at **MEDIUM** 4½ to 5½ minutes or until scalded. Quickly stir in eggs, sugar and vanilla. Pour into 6 greased custard cups (6 oz. ea.); sprinkle with nutmeg. On glass oven tray, arrange dishes in circular pattern. Cook at **MEDIUM-LOW** 9 to 11 minutes. Rearrange custard cups every three minutes. Remove custards as they are cooked. Custards are cooked when they are firmly set about 1-inch from edge, and center is thickened but not set. Center will set as custard cools.
Let stand until cool.

Variation:
For CARAMEL CUSTARD, *in small glass bowl, cook ½ cup sugar and 3 tablespoons water at **HIGH** 4 to 5 minutes or until sugar is melted and light brown. Pour into greased custard cups, tilting cups to coat bottom. Proceed as directed above.*

217

APPLE BETTY I-M

4 cups peeled, cored, apple slices (about 4 to 5 medium)
2 tablespoons sugar
2 tablespoons lemon juice
½ cup old-fashioned or quick oats
⅔ cup packed brown sugar
1 teaspoon cinnamon
1 teaspoon nutmeg
⅓ cup butter or margarine
½ cup chopped walnuts

Yield: 6 Servings

Arrange apple slices in a greased 8-inch round dish. Sprinkle with sugar and lemon juice. Combine oats, brown sugar, cinnamon and nutmeg; cut in butter until mixture resembles coarse crumbs. Add nuts; mix. Crumble mixture over apple slices.

TO COOK BY INSTA-MATIC: Cover completley with plastic wrap. Cook on **COOK 6**.

TO COOK BY TIME: Cook at **MEDIUM** 20 minutes.

TO COMPLETE: Let stand, uncovered, 5 minutes.

BAKED APPLES I-M

4 large baking apples (about 6 oz. ea.)
¼ cup packed brown sugar
2 tablespoons finely chopped nuts or raisins
¼ teaspoon cinnamon
2 tablespoons butter or margarine
¼ cup water

Yield: 4 Servings

Core apples, leaving small plug in blossom end; peel skin 1-inch from top. Combine sugar, nuts and cinnamon; fill apples with mixture.
Arrange apples in 8-inch square dish. Dot with butter and sprinkle with water. Cover completely with plastic wrap.

TO COOK BY INSTA-MATIC: Cook on **COOK 8**.

TO COOK BY TIME: Cook at **HIGH** 6 minutes.

TO COMPLETE: After cooking, release plastic wrap. Let stand, covered, 5 minutes; serve warm or chilled, spooning sauce over apples.

Note: For TWO Servings, follow above procedure. Halve all ingredients. Cook apples 3 to 4 minutes.
For ONE Serving, cook apples 1½ to 2 minutes.

CHUNKY APPLESAUCE I-M

3 pounds baking apples, peeled, cored and sliced (about 5½ cups)
¾ cup sugar or to taste
½ cup water
½ to 1 teaspoon cinnamon

Yield: 5½ Cups

Combine all ingredients in large glass bowl.

TO COOK BY INSTA-MATIC: Cover completely with plastic wrap. Cook on **COOK 8**. After cooking, release plastic wrap.

TO COOK BY TIME: Cover with wax paper. Cook at **HIGH** 7 to 10 minutes, or until apples are tender stir once.

TO COMPLETE: Let stand, covered, 7 minutes. Mash apples until chunky; serve warm or chilled.

CARAMEL APPLES

1 package (14 oz.) caramels
1 tablespoon hot water
4 to 5 medium apples
Wooden ice cream sticks
Finely chopped nuts

Yield: 4–5 Servings

Combine caramels and water in a 1-quart glass measure. Cook at **HIGH** 2 to 3 minutes, or until melted; stir twice until smooth. Insert sticks into stem of apples. Dip each apple into caramel mixture turning and tipping dish to coat apples; sprinkle with chopped nuts. Place on greased waxed paper lined cookie sheet. Store in a cool place.

*Tip: If caramel mixture becomes too stiff while dipping apples, return to oven and cook at **HIGH** ½ to ¾ minute.*

FRUIT COBBLER

Filling:
2 cans (30 oz. ea.) peach slices or other canned fruit*,
    drained (reserve ¼ cup syrup)
3 tablespoons flour
½ tablespoon lemon juice
½ teaspoon vanilla
½ teaspoon cinnamon

Topping:
1 cup buttermilk biscuit mix
¼ cup packed brown sugar
¼ cup butter or margarine, softened (see page 234)
2 tablespoons hot water

Yield: 6 Servings

Combine Filling ingredients in 8-inch square dish. Combine topping ingredients, stir until dough pulls away from sides of bowl and forms a ball. Gently spread topping onto filling (topping will spread slightly when heated). Sprinkle, if desired, with additional cinnamon. Cook at **MEDIUM-HIGH** 9 to 11 minutes, or until topping is set.
Let stand to cool.

*Variations:
For FRESH PEACH Cobbler, combine 1½ pounds peeled and sliced peaches and ¼ to ⅓ cup packed brown sugar; cook, covered, at **HIGH** 3½ to 4 minutes or until tender. Follow above procedure, omitting ¼ cup reserved syrup.
For QUICK Fruit Cobbler, substitute 2 cans (21 oz. ea.) fruit pie filling and ¼ cup water for Filling ingredients.*

CURRIED FRUIT COMPOTE

1 can (17 oz.) apricot halves, drained;
  reserve syrup
1 can (16 oz.) peach slices, drained;
  reserve syrup
¼ teaspoon curry powder
¼ teaspoon cinnamon
1 tablespoon cornstarch
¼ cup water
½ cup raisins

Yield: 6 Servings

In 2-cup glass measure, combine 1 cup
reserved syrups, curry and cinnamon. Cook
at **HIGH** 2 to 3 minutes. Blend cornstarch
with water until smooth. Stir into syrup.
Cook at **HIGH** 1½ to 2 minutes, or until
slightly thickened; stir occasionally. In 8-
inch round dish, combine apricots,
peaches and raisins. Cook at **HIGH** 3½ to
4½ minutes, or until heated through, stir
once. Pour sauce over fruit. Cook at **HIGH**
1 to 1½ minutes.
Serve warm or chilled.

BAKED GRAPEFRUIT

2 medium grapefruit
8 teaspoons packed brown sugar,
  granulated sugar or maple syrup
Cinnamon

Yield: 4 Servings

With sharp knife, cut each grapefruit in
half; remove seeds and cut around each
section. Arrange grapefruit on glass oven
tray. Sprinkle with brown sugar. Cook at
HIGH 3½ to 4½ minutes. Sprinkle with
cinnamon before serving.

Note: **For TWO Servings,** *follow above*
procedure. Halve all ingredients;
cook 2 to 3 minutes.
For ONE Serving, *cook 1 to 2*
minutes.

PEARS IN WINE SAUCE I-M

2 cinnamon sticks
¼ cup sugar
½ teaspoon whole cloves
¼ teaspoon grated lemon peel
½ cup port wine
2 tablespoons water
2 tablespoons apricot preserves
2 tablespoons apricot brandy
6 small pears, halved lengthwise, peeled,
  cored

Yield: 6 Servings

Combine cinnamon, sugar, cloves, lemon,
wine, water, preserves and brandy. Arrange
pears, cut-side down in 8-inch round dish.
Pour sauce over pears. Cover completely
with plastic wrap.

TO COOK BY INSTA-MATIC: Cook on
COOK 8.

TO COOK BY TIME: Cook at **HIGH** 8 to 9
minutes.

TO COMPLETE: After cooking, release
plastic wrap. Let stand, covered, 5
minutes. To serve; baste pears with sauce.
Remove cinnamon stick and cloves before
serving.

BRANDIED PEACHES

**1 can (29 oz.) cling-peach halves, drained;
  (reserve ½ cup syrup)**
⅔ cup peach or pineapple preserves
¼ to ⅓ cup brandy
1 teaspoon lemon juice
Toasted coconut (see page 233)

Yield: 4 Servings

Arrange peaches in 8-inch round dish.
Combine reserved syrup, preserves, brandy
and lemon juice. Pour over peaches; top
with coconut. Cover with plastic wrap.
Cook at **HIGH** 3 to 4 minutes, or until
heated through. Serve warm or chilled.

FRUIT TART

1½ cups flour*
½ cup oil
2 tablespoons milk
1 tablespoon sugar
1 teaspoon salt
**½ cup apricot, peach or favorite preserves,
  divided**
Sliced fresh or canned fruit, well drained

Yield: 4 Servings

Combine flour, oil, milk, sugar and salt; put
onto bottom and sides of 9-inch pie plate;
set aside. Heat 3 tablespoons preserves in
small glass bowl at **HIGH** 10 to 15 seconds,
or until melted; stir. Brush tart shell with
preserves. Pierce shell with fork; Cook at
HIGH 4½ to 5 minutes; cool. Heat
remaining preserves at **HIGH** ½ minute,
or until melted. Arrange, fruit on tart shell;
brush with preserves. Cut into wedges to
serve.
***Substitution:** Use ¾ cup whole wheat
flour and ¾ cup all-purpose flour for 1½
cups.

PEARS WITH CARAMEL SAUCE

6 large pears (6 oz. ea.)
1 tablespoon sugar
Dash cinnamon
½ cup water
30 caramels (about 10 oz.)
2 tablespoons butter or margarine
2 tablespoons rum, optional
1 tablespoon water
½ teaspoon cinnamon
Sweetened whipped cream

Yield: 6 Servings

Core pears and peel skin 1 inch from top.
Combine sugar and dash cinnamon;
sprinkle inside pears.
Arrange pears in 12×8-inch dish. Sprinkle
with water. Cook, covered with plastic
wrap, at **HIGH** 8 to 9 minutes, or until
pears are tender, cool or chill.
Just before serving, in glass bowl,
combine caramels, butter, rum, water and
cinnamon. Cook at **HIGH** 2 to 3 minutes,
stir twice until smooth.
Spoon sauce over pears; top with whipped
cream.

PREPARING PIE CRUSTS

Prepare pastry according to recipe or package directions.

If desired, for a single crust homemade pastry recipe, substitute ½ cup whole wheat flour for ½ cup all-purpose flour.

Microwave pie crusts are light in color. A few drops of yellow food coloring may be mixed with the liquid before adding liquid to the flour mixture. This will give the crust a pale yellow color.

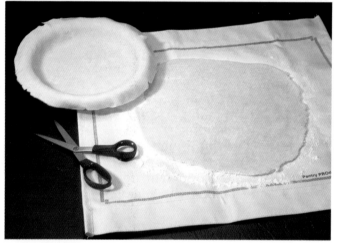

Roll dough out and gently place in pie plate. Trim edge so a ¾-inch overhang remains.
Fold under extra pastry to buid up edge of crust. Flute edge.

Prick bottom and sides of pastry with fork. Let pie crust rest 10 minutes. The rest time helps reduce shrinkage.

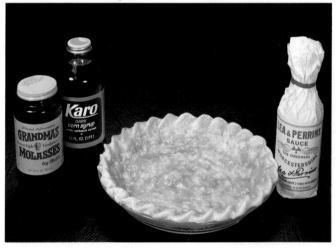

If desired, brush with dark corn syrup or molasses for sweet fillings, or brush with Worcestershire or soy sauce for savory fillings.

CRUMB CRUSTS

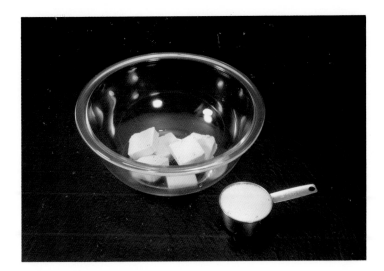

For crumb crusts combine ⅓ cup butter and ¼ cup sugar in glass bowl.

Heat until butter is melted. Combine with 1¼ cups crumbs (graham crackers, chocolate or vanilla wafers).

Firmly pat into 9-inch pie plate.

For frozen crust, defrost and remove from foil pie plate. Place in an 8 or 9-inch glass pie plate.

Cook ½ minute, then prick crust and, if desired, brush with dark corn syrup, molasses, Worcestershire or soy sauce.

Cook according to directions given in chart. Visually check for doneness. Pastry crusts should be opaque. If crust is undercooked, add cooking time in 15 second increments. Let stand until cool. Chill crumb crusts.

BAKING PIE CRUSTS

ITEM	POWER	APPROX. COOKING TIME (in minutes)
Homemade or Mix	HIGH	3½ to 5
Frozen	HIGH	4 to 5½
Graham Cracker or Cookie Crumb	MEDIUM	2 to 2½

FRESH PEACH PIE

2 pounds fresh peaches, peeled and
   sliced*
½ cup packed brown sugar
2 teaspoons lemon juice
1½ teaspoon cornstarch
½ teaspoon cinnamon, optional
9-inch pastry shell, baked (see page 222)

Crumb Topping:
½ cup flour
⅓ cup packed brown sugar
¼ cup butter or margarine, softened
   (see page 234)
⅓ cup finely chopped nuts, optional
¼ teaspoon cinnamon

Yield: 8 Servings

Toss peaches with sugar, lemon juice,
cornstarch and cinnamon; arrange in
prepared shell. Cook, covered with wax
paper, at **HIGH** 4 to 6 minutes, or until
peaches are almost tender.
Meanwhile, prepare crumb topping. In
bowl, combine flour, brown sugar, butter,
nuts and cinnamon.
Sprinkle pie with crumb topping. Cook at
HIGH 4 to 5 minutes, or until topping is
set. Cool.

*Variation: For FRESH APPLE PIE, use 2
   pounds apples in place of
   peaches.*

ORANGE MANDARIN CHIFFON PIE

1 envelope unflavored gelatin
⅓ cup sugar
4 eggs, separated
1 can (11 oz.) mandarin orange sections,
   drained; reserve ⅔ cup syrup
2 tablespoons lemon juice
½ teaspoon grated lemon peel
½ cup sugar
9-inch graham cracker crumb crust, baked
   (see page 223)

Yield: 6 Servings

In medium glass bowl, mix gelatin and ⅓
cup sugar; stir in egg yolks blended with
reserved syrup, lemon juice and lemon
peel. Cook at **MEDIUM-HIGH** 5 to 6
minutes, or until gelatin is dissolved; stir
twice.
Chill until mixture mounds slightly, stir
occasionally.
Meanwhile, beat egg whites until soft
peaks form; gradually add ½ cup sugar
and beat until stiff. Fold in gelatin mixture
and ½ oranges; turn into prepared crust.
Chill until firm; garnish with remaining
oranges.

CRANBERRY NUT PIE

1 pound cranberries, coarsely chopped
1½ cups sugar
⅛ teaspoon salt
½ cup coarsely chopped walnuts
½ cup raisins
1 teaspoon orange peel
3 tablespoons butter or margarine, melted
1½ tablespoons cornstarch
½ cup water
¼ cup orange juice
9-inch graham cracker crust, baked
  (see page 223)
Sweetened whipped cream or
  whipped topping

Yield: 8 Servings

In 2½ quart bowl, mix cranberries, sugar and salt. Stir in nuts, raisins, peel and butter. Mix cornstarch with water and juice; stir into cranberry mixture. Cook at **HIGH** 12 to 14 minutes, or until mixture thickens. Stir occasionally. Pour into crust; chill. To serve, top with sweetened whipped cream.

GREAT GRAPE PIE

1 envelope unflavored gelatin
¾ cup water
1 can (6 oz.) frozen grape juice concentrate
1 cup heavy cream, whipped
9-inch graham cracker crumb crust, baked*
  (see page 223)
Sugared grape clusters, optional

Yield: 8 Servings

In large glass bowl, sprinkle unflavored gelatin over water. Cook at **HIGH** 1¼ to 1¾ minutes, or until gelatin is dissolved; stir twice. Stir in grape juice concentrate until melted; chill until mixture mounds slightly, stir occasionally. Fold in whipped cream; turn into prepared crust and chill until firm. Garnish, if desired, with sugared grape clusters.

Hint: *When preparing ingredients for crust, add ¼ cup finely chopped nuts and ¼ teaspoon each allspice, cinnamon and nutmeg.*

ORCHARD FRUIT PIE

1 can (21 oz.) favorite pie filling
¼ cup raisins, optional
1 teaspoon lemon or orange juice
⅛ teaspoon cinnamon
8 or 9-inch pastry shell, baked
  (see page 222)
½ cup flour
¼ cup brown sugar
¼ cup butter or margarine, softened
  (see page 234)

Yield: 8 Servings

Combine pie filling, raisins, lemon juice and cinnamon; pour into prepared crust. Blend together remaining ingredients; crumble over filling. Cook at **MEDIUM-HIGH** 6 to 8 minutes, or until heated through. Cool before serving.

GRASSHOPPER PIE

3 cups miniature marshmallows
½ cup milk or half'n half
3 tablespoons creme de cocoa
3 tablespoons creme de menthe
1 cup heavy cream, whipped
9-inch chocolate cookie crumb crust, baked
   (see page 223)

Yield: 8 Servings

Combine marshmallows and milk in large glass bowl. Cook at **MEDIUM** 3½ to 4½ minutes; stir until smooth. Stir in creme de cocoa and creme de menthe; chill until mixture mounds slightly. Fold in whipped cream and turn into prepared crust. Chill until firm.

COCONUT LEMON MERINGUE I-M PIE

1½ cups sugar
⅓ cup cornstarch
¼ teaspoon salt
1 cups boiling water
3 eggs, separated
½ cup lemon juice
3 tablespoons butter or margarine
Grated peel of 1 lemon
9-inch pie shell, baked (see page 222)
⅓ cup sugar
¼ cup toasted coconut (see page 233)

Yield: 8 Servings

In 3-quart glass casserole, combine 1½ cups sugar, cornstarch and salt; stir in boiling water.

TO COOK BY INSTA-MATIC: Cover with lid. Cook on **COOK 3.**

TO COOK BY TIME: Cover with lid. Cook at **HIGH** 9 to 10 minutes, or until thickened. Halfway through cooking, stir once.

TO COMPLETE: Stir in small amount of hot mixture into egg yolks; return to hot mixture, beating until well blended. Add lemon juice, butter and lemon peel. Pour into pie shell; set aside.
Meanwhile, beat egg whites until soft peaks form, gradually add remaining sugar and beat until stiff. Spread meringue over filling, making sure it touches crust all around. Sprinkle with coconut. Cook at **HIGH** 3 to 4 minutes, or until meringue is set. Cool completely.

CHOCOLATE ROCKY ROAD PIE

1 package (3⅝ oz.) chocolate pudding and
   pie filling mix
1¾ cups milk
1 to 1½ cups miniature marshmallows
½ to 1 cup coarsely chopped walnuts
9-inch chocolate cookie crumb crust, baked
 (see chart on page 223)

Yield: 8 Servings

Combine pudding mix and milk in 4-cup glass measure. Cook at **MEDIUM** 7 to 8½ minutes, or until pudding is thickened; stir twice. Cool 5 minutes; fold in marshmallows and nuts.
Turn into prepared crust; chill until firm.

PUMPKIN PIE

1 can (16 oz.) cooked pumpkin
1 cup evaporated milk
2 eggs
½ cup sugar
¼ cup packed brown sugar
½ teaspoon salt
1 teaspoon cinnamon
½ teaspoon ginger
¼ teaspoon cloves
9-inch pastry shell, baked (see page 222)

Yield: 8 Servings

Combine pumpkin, milk, eggs, sugar, salt and spices. Pour into prepared shell. Cook at **MEDIUM** 20 to 22 minutes, or until center is almost set. Let stand until cool.

PECAN PIE

1 cup dark corn syrup
¼ cup packed brown sugar
3 eggs
2 tablespoons butter or margarine, melted
1 teaspoon vanilla
¾ cup chopped pecans
9-inch pastry shell, baked (see page 222)
Sweetened whipped cream, optional

Yield: 8 Servings

Combine syrup, sugar, eggs, butter and vanilla; stir in pecans. Pour into prepared crust. Cook at **MEDIUM** 7 to 9 minutes, or until pie is set. Let stand until cool. Garnish, if desired, with sweetened whipped cream.

MAMA'S CHESS PIE

1 cup packed brown sugar
½ cup sugar
3 eggs
½ cup evaporated milk
½ cup chopped walnuts, optional
1 teaspoon vanilla extract
⅛ teaspoon lemon extract
9-inch pastry shell, baked (see page 222)
Sweetened whipped cream

Yield: 8 Servings

Combine sugar, eggs, milk, walnuts, and extracts; pour into prepared shell. Cook at **MEDIUM** 8½ to 10 minutes, or until center is almost set. Let stand until cool. Just before serving, top with whipped cream.

PEANUT BRITTLE

1 cup sugar
½ cup light corn syrup
1 cup salted peanuts
1 teaspoon butter or margarine
1 teaspoon vanilla
1 teaspoon baking soda

Yield: 1½ Pounds

In 2-quart glass measure combine sugar and corn syrup; stir. Cook at **HIGH** 4 minutes. Add peanuts; stir well. Cook for an additional 3½ minutes; add butter and vanilla, stirring well. Cook 1½ minutes. Add baking soda; stir gently until light and foamy. Immediately pour mixture onto buttered cookie sheet. Spread thinly. Cool; break into small pieces.

POPPY COCK

½ cup butter or margarine
1 cup packed brown sugar
¼ cup light corn syrup
½ teaspoon baking soda
1 cup peanuts, walnut or pecan
   halves, or combination
8 cups popped popcorn

Yield: 9 Cups

In 3-quart glass bowl, combine butter, sugar and syrup. Cook at **HIGH** 3 minutes; stir. Add baking soda, stir gently until light and foamy. Cook 1½ minutes; stir in nuts. Add popcorn (unpopped kernels removed); stir until well coated. Cook 1½ minutes. Spread mixture onto buttered wax paper; let stand at room temperature 1 hour to harden. Loosen mixture from wax paper; break into pieces.

CARAMEL COCONUT BALLS

28 caramels (about 8 oz.)
¼ cup butter or margarine
2 tablespoons half 'n half or milk
1½ cups confectioners sugar, sifted
1 cup salted peanuts
2 cups miniature marshmallows
1 cup flaked coconut

Yield: 3½ Dozen

In 2-quart glass measure, place caramels, butter and half 'n half. Cook at **HIGH** 5 minutes, or until melted and smooth, stirring after 3 minutes. Stir in sugar until smooth; add peanuts. Stir in marshmallows just until lightly coated. Shape caramel mixture into balls; roll in coconut until well coated. Store in covered container.

PEPPERMINT BARK

1 pound white chocolate (candy coating)
¾ cup crushed peppermint candy

Yield: 1 Pound

Break white chocolate into pieces; place in single layer in 2-quart glass bowl. Cook at **MEDIUM** 5 to 6 minutes; stir once. Stir in peppermint candy. Pour immediately onto ungreased cookie sheet; spread to ¼-inch thickness. Cool until firm; break into pieces. Store in covered container.

Variation:
For ALMOND BARK, *add ⅔ cup sliced almonds in place of peppermint candy.*

BUTTERSCOTCH FUDGE

3 cups sugar
¾ cup butter or margarine
1 can (5⅓ oz.) evaporated milk
1 package (12 oz.) butterscotch flavored
  pieces*
1 jar (7½ oz.) marshmallow creme
1 cup chopped walnuts
1 teaspoon vanilla

Yield: 3 Pounds

In 2½-quart casserole, combine sugar,
butter and milk. Cook at **HIGH** 9 to 10½
minutes, or until sugar is dissolved; stir
twice. Add remaining ingredients and stir
until butterscotch is melted. Turn into well
greased 12×8-inch dish. Cool; cut into
squares to serve.

Variation:
  For CHOCOLATE Fudge, use 1 package
  (12 oz.) semisweet chocolate pieces.

FAST FIXIN' CHOCOLATE FUDGE

2 packages (16 oz. ea.) confectioners sugar
1 cup unsweetened cocoa
½ cup milk
1 cup butter or margarine
1½ cups chopped nuts, optional
2 tablespoons vanilla

Yield: 3 Pounds

Mix sugar and cocoa in large glass bowl.
Add milk and butter (do not stir). Cook at
HIGH 4½ to 6 minutes, or until butter is
melted; add nuts and vanilla; stir until
smooth. Spread into well greased 12×8-
inch dish. Chill until firm. Cut into squares
to serve.

Note: For 1½ pounds Fudge, *follow above*
  procedure. Halve all ingredients
  cook 2 to 3 minutes; pour into
  greased 8-inch square dish.

Variation:
For ROCKY ROAD Fudge, *coarsely chop*
nuts and add 1 cup miniature
marshmallows.

PECAN PRALINES

1 cup packed brown sugar
1 cup granulated sugar
⅓ cup light corn syrup
¼ cup water
1½ cups coarsely chopped pecans
1 tablespoon butter or margarine
1 teaspoon vanilla

Yield: 1½ Dozen

In medium glass bowl, combine sugars, corn syrup and water. Cook at **HIGH** 7 to 9 minutes, or until mixture reads 238°F (soft ball stage) when tested with candy thermometer*. Stir in pecans, butter and vanilla. Let stand 2 minutes.
Drop by tablespoonfuls onto well greased wax paper lined cookie sheet; chill until set.

***Important:** Do not use conventional candy thermometer in dish while operating the microwave oven.*

TOFFEE FONDUE

1 package (14 oz.) caramels
¼ cup strong coffee
2 to 4 tablespoons milk
½ cup milk chocolate pieces, optional
Dippers*

Yield: 6 Servings

In medium glass bowl, combine caramels, coffee, milk and chocolate. Cook at **MEDIUM** 5 to 6 minutes; stir twice until smooth.
Serve with assorted Dippers. If Fondue gets cool, reheat 1 to 2 minutes.

***Dippers:** Apple and pear slices, banana chunks, large marshmallows, angel food or yellow cake, cut into 1½-inch cubes.*

ALMOND BUTTER CRUNCH

½ cup butter or margarine
1½ cups sugar
3 tablespoons water
1 tablespoon light corn syrup
4 (1⅕ oz. ea.) milk chocolate candy bars
½ cup finely chopped almonds

Yield: 1¼ Pounds

Heat butter in 3-quart glass ceramic casserole at **HIGH** 1½ to 2 minutes, or until melted; stir in sugar, water and corn syrup. Cook at **HIGH** 8 to 9 minutes, or until mixture reads 290°F (soft crack stage) when tested with candy thermometer*. Pour onto well greased wax paper; let stand ½ minute.
Arrange chocolate on candy; as chocolate melts, spread evenly over candy. Top with nuts, pressing nuts into chocolate. Chill until chocolate is set; break into small pieces.

***Important:** Do not use conventional candy thermometer in dish while operating the microwave oven.*

231

RAISIN CLUSTERS

8 squares (1 oz. ea.) semi-sweet chocolate
⅔ cup sweetened condensed milk
1 cup raisins*

Yield: 2 Dozen

In medium glass bowl, cook chocolate at **MEDIUM-LOW** 3 to 4 minutes, or until chocolate is melted; stir in milk until smooth, then raisins. Drop by teaspoonfuls onto greased wax paper lined cookie sheet; chill.

***Variations:**
 For CHINESE Clusters, use 1 cup crisp chow mein noodles for raisins.
 For ELEPHANT Clusters, use 1 cup unsalted peanuts for raisins.

SWEET SPICED NUTS

½ cup packed brown sugar
1½ tablespoons water
½ teaspoon salt
½ teaspoon cinnamon
¼ teaspoon allspice
⅛ teaspoon cloves
⅛ teaspoon nutmeg
1½ cups almond, cashew, pecan or walnut halves or
  combination

Yield: 1½ Cups

In 2-quart casserole, combine sugar, water, salt, cinnamon, allspice, cloves and nutmeg. Cook at **HIGH** 1 to 1½ minutes, or until sugar is melted; stir in nuts. Cook at **HIGH** 3½ to 4½ minutes, or until syrup begins to harden. Immediately pour nut mixture onto buttered cookie sheet. Spread thinly. Cool; break into small pieces.

MICROWAVE SHORTCUTS

To further illustrate the versatility of your microwave oven, here are some of our favorite tips to help you save more time.

Because all times given are approximate and may vary do not leave the oven unattended.

To Soften Dried Fruits, place fruit in a small bowl and sprinkle with water. Cover with plastic wrap and heat at **HIGH** 30 to 40 seconds.

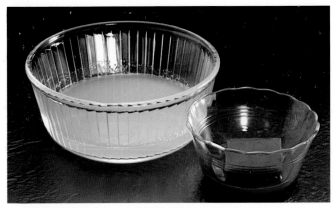

To Melt Butter or Chocolate place ¼ pound butter or 1 square (1 oz.) chocolate in dish. Heat butter 1 to 2 minutes and chocolate 2 to 3 minutes at **MEDIUM-LOW**. Check before adding more time.

To Toast Coconut, spread ⅓ cup coconut in a 9-inch pie plate. Heat at **HIGH** 1 to 1½ minutes, or until golden brown; stir twice.

To Remove Oven Odors, combine water with the juice and peel of one lemon in a small bowl. Heat at **HIGH** 5 minutes; wipe oven interior with damp cloth.

To Dry Herbs, place a few sprigs or ½ cup leaves between paper towels. Heat at **HIGH** 1 to 1½ minutes or until dry and crumbly. Check frequently. Timings may vary with different herbs.

To Dry Lemon or Orange Peel, place grated peel in glass bowl. Heat at **HIGH** 30 to 60 seconds, or until dry; stir once.

233

To Soften Cream Cheese (3 oz. package) or ¼ pound of Butter, remove from wrapper and place on a dish. Heat at **LOW** 30 to 60 seconds.

To Reheat a Slice of Cold Fruit Pie, place on a dish. Heat at **MEDIUM-HIGH** 15 to 45 seconds.

To Reheat an 8 oz. Baby Bottle of cold milk or formula to lukewarm, remove cap and nipple from bottle. Heat at **MEDIUM** 30 to 60 seconds. Screw nipple on bottle, gently shake bottle and let stand 1 to 2 minutes before using. Do not heat bottles with disposable linings in the microwave oven.

To Shorten Barbecue Cooking Time, partially cook chicken, ribs, etc. in the microwave oven. Then season and finish cooking on a barbecue grill.

Cook Chicken pieces at **HIGH** when you need chicken for salad, sandwiches or casseroles. One pound of chicken should cook 7 to 8 minutes.

To Separate Cold Bacon, heat package at **HIGH** 15 to 30 seconds.

To Soften Hard Ice Cream, heat a half-gallon at **WARM** 3½ to 5 minutes.

To Heat Liqueurs for Flaming Desserts, place ¼ cup liqueur in glass measure. Heat at **HIGH** 20 to 30 seconds. Pour over dessert and ignite.

To Roast Nuts, place 1½ cups nuts in 9-inch glass pie plate. Heat at **HIGH** for 3 to 4 minutes; stir twice.

To Toast Sesame Seeds, place ¼ cup of sesame seeds in a small bowl. Heat at **HIGH** for 2½ to 3½ minutes; stir twice.

To Make Croutons, cut enough dry bread to make 2 cups of bread cubes. Spread cubes in a shallow dish. Cook at **HIGH** 3 to 4 minutes; stir occasionally.

To Soften Brown Sugar, place 1 cup hard brown sugar in dish with a slice of bread or a wedge of apple. Cover with plastic wrap. Heat at **HIGH** 30 to 60 seconds.

INDEX

237

239

241

242

X40AQ (84.5)
Printed in Japan